50+ App Features with Python

Implement feature-focused, code-driven Python capabilities with UX at the core

AF527385

Ylena Zorak

Copyright © 2025 by GitforGits

All rights reserved. This book is protected under copyright laws and no part of it may be reproduced or transmitted in any form or by any means, electronic or mechanical, including photocopying, recording, or by any information storage and retrieval system, without the prior written permission of the publisher. Any unauthorized reproduction, distribution, or transmission of this work may result in civil and criminal penalties and will be dealt with in the respective jurisdiction at anywhere in India, in accordance with the applicable copyright laws.

Published by: GitforGits

Publisher: Sonal Dhandre

www.gitforgits.com

support@gitforgits.com

Printed in India

First Printing: February 2025

ISBN: 978-93-49174-15-3

Cover Design by: Kitten Publishing

For permission to use material from this book, please contact GitforGits at support@gitforgits.com.

Prologue

These days, people expect a lot from the software we build. As users, we don't just look for apps to solve one problem; we want to feel comfortable, be fast, and feel secure. We also want to see that the app was made by someone who knows what they're doing. We measure the success of every new product launch, every upgrade, and even the smallest feature release by how well it makes our daily life easier, smoother, or more delightful. This pressure isn't just about business success. It's about the satisfaction I get when someone says, "That feature just works—better than I hoped."

When I started out as a Python developer, I began with small, simple scripts. But as my projects grew, it became clear that people's expectations were changing quickly. They were after more than just working code. They wanted features that anticipate needs, interfaces that feel natural, and tools that keep them in control. They expected secure logins, instant feedback, drag-and-drop uploads, dark mode toggles, and seamless integration with their favorite services. They wanted it all to feel easy. That challenge excited me. I saw an opportunity to step beyond the basics and start putting together real solutions—features that could power not just the next prototype, but production-ready apps with real users and real demands. I'm into Python not as a way to automate stuff or do analysis, but more as a way to build super compelling, modern software experiences.

Writing this book was my way of sharing everything I'd learned about building applications that meet those high expectations. I wrote every chapter so that we could build something together. I wanted to show, not just explain, how to take an idea and turn it into something that's ready to use in your own projects. I give practical, hands-on examples for every feature I cover. These examples solve real problems and can stand up to production scrutiny.

From the start such as, setting up our Linux development environment, organizing code with reproducible workflows, and picking the right libraries, I make sure we're focused on productivity and long-term success. I'll teach you to craft strong APIs with FastAPI, use Pydantic and SQLAlchemy for data integrity, and apply patterns that avoid repetition. As we go through CRUD operations, advanced pagination, filtering, and bulk data handling, you'll see that each concept builds on what came before. You'll learn to add features and connect them into a smooth whole. You'll find step-by-step instructions for secure authentication, password resets, role-based permissions, and even two-factor authentication. When we talk about user experience, I show you to implement dynamic forms, drag-and-drop uploads, custom error pages, and theme toggles. You'll learn to bring external services into your app, like sending emails, integrating SMS, or allowing users to log in with Google or GitHub.

When it's time to deploy, I'll show you to use Docker for containerization and Kubernetes for orchestration. I'll also cover real-world patterns for logging, monitoring, and scaling. We've got CSRF and CORS protections, data encryption, content security policies, and append-only audit logging. I make sure you're comfortable with Pytest, writing both unit and integration tests, and using GitHub Actions to automate linting, builds, and coverage reporting. You'll walk away with a CI/CD pipeline that'll put your mind at ease every time you push code.

I wrote this book for developers who want practical solutions, clear patterns, and the confidence to ship features that users love.

--Ylena Zorak

Content

Preface

"50+ App Features with Python" is for developers who want to build real solutions, not just read theory. The book will help you work with robust, feature-centric code that brings today's most popular app capabilities to life. This includes core data management and authentication, rich user experiences, notification systems, security layers, deployment, and modern testing pipelines.

To get started, you'll set up your development environment and dive right into building APIs with FastAPI, making sure your data is validated with Pydantic, and checking out database management using SQLAlchemy. You'll get access to advanced features like CRUD endpoints, pagination, filtering, and bulk import/export without having to go back and relearn the basics. We'll go over how to set up authentication and authorization flows, including role-based access and two-factor authentication, in the context of secure, maintainable code. It then goes on to user-centric enhancements, showing how to implement drag-and-drop uploads, dynamic forms, custom error pages, and adaptive themes. Basically, it brings real interactivity to your projects.

When it comes to hands-on experience, you'll be using real integrations like Celery for background tasks, Twilio for SMS, OAuth2 for social login, and webhook handling for event-driven workflows. Once it's time to deploy, you'll learn about containerization with Docker, orchestration with Kubernetes, log aggregation, and operational monitoring. Security and compliance are a big deal here, with heavy coverage of CSRF, CORS, encryption, CSP headers, and audit logging. The last few chapters are all about testing and CI/CD. You'll learn about unit and integration testing with Pytest, pipeline automation with GitHub Actions, and coverage reporting.

This book will help you level up your Python skills and get a better understanding of high-impact libraries. While it's not a roadmap to mastering every app capability, it's designed to give you hands-on experience and the confidence to build features you really want in your app.

In this book, you will learn to:

- Set up Python environments with reproducible workflows.
- Use FastAPI, Pydantic, and SQLAlchemy to build RESTful APIs.
- Implement CRUD, pagination, filtering, and scalable API endpoints.
- Develop authentication, password resets, roles, and two-factor security.
- Create interactive forms, uploads, error pages, and theme toggles.
- Integrate email, SMS, social logins, and webhook handling.
- Use Docker Compose and Kubernetes manifests to make it scalable.
- Secure your apps with CSRF, CORS, AES-GCM, and CSP headers.
- Monitor user actions with tamper-proof, timestamped audit trails.
- Use Pytest and GitHub Actions to automate testing and coverage.

GitforGits

Prerequisites

This book is designed and meticulously curate for developers, programmers, app specialists who are keen to bring the attractive and the most functional features to their apps with simple python scripts and easy-to-use libraries. All you need to know is basic programming skills of Python before you start with this book.

Codes Usage

Are you in need of some helpful code examples to assist you in our programming and documentation? Look no further! Our book offers a wealth of supplemental material, including code examples and exercises.

Not only is this book here to aid you in getting our job done, but you have our permission to use the example code in our programs and documentation. However, please note that if you are reproducing a significant portion of the code, we do require you to contact us for permission.

But don't worry, using several chunks of code from this book in our program or answering a question by citing our book and quoting example code does not require permission. But if you do choose to give credit, an attribution typically includes the title, author, publisher, and ISBN. For example, "50+ App Features with Python by Ylena Zorak".

If you are unsure whether our intended use of the code examples falls under fair use or the permissions outlined above, please do not hesitate to reach out to us at support@gitforgits.com.

We are happy to assist and clarify any concerns.

Acknowledgement

I owe a tremendous debt of gratitude to GitforGits, for their unflagging enthusiasm and wise counsel throughout the entire process of writing this book. Their knowledge and careful editing helped make sure the piece was useful for people of all reading levels and comprehension skills. In addition, I'd like to thank everyone involved in the publishing process for their efforts in making this book a reality. Their efforts, from copyediting to advertising, made the project what it is today.

Finally, I'd like to express my gratitude to everyone who has shown me unconditional love and encouragement throughout my life. Their support was crucial to the completion of this book. I appreciate our help with this endeavour and our continued interest in my career.

CHAPTER 1: ENVIRONMENT SETUP & CORE DATA MANAGEMENT

Overview

In this first chapter, we're going to set up a solid base for all the advanced features we'll be adding later on by creating a consistent and powerful development environment. First, we'll set up Python 3.11 on Ubuntu and build an isolated virtual environment. This'll let us manage dependencies efficiently. We'll introduce the core libraries that'll support the whole project and create a scalable structure for our codebase. We're going to build a basic data model, design service patterns, and develop our first RESTful CRUD endpoints using FastAPI and Pydantic. This'll help us get data validation and error handling down pat. We'll be adding pagination and metadata to our endpoints so we can handle and navigate big datasets like a pro. You'll learn how to set up advanced filtering and dynamic sorting, so clients can make precise queries with minimal effort. Finally, it'll walk you through creating strong bulk import and export tools for both CSV and JSON, and incorporate streaming to deal with large data transfers. By the time you're done, you'll know how to build, safeguard, and expand the core data layer of any modern app, all while getting ready for the tricky features that are coming up.

Environment Configuration

A well-thought-out environment sets the stage for a successful software project. When you're working with a modern language like Python, the choices you make at the start can really affect how easy and reliable the whole development process is. In this book, we're going to focus on building practical features that power real-world applications. We're going to build more than fifty different and widely-used application capabilities, and each one will contribute to a complete and versatile codebase. So, as we start working together, the first thing we'll do is set up a stable and repeatable setup on Ubuntu 22.04 LTS. That way, we can be sure that all future developments will be consistent and predictable.

We're here to make sure you've got all the info you need and that everything goes smoothly. If we plan and set up our workspace right, we can avoid a lot of environmental issues that might mess with our learning or slow down our progress. When you've got a solid foundation, you can focus on the logic and problem-solving aspects of building applications instead of dealing with dependencies or conflicts. We'll be using the same environment and workflow throughout, so each new feature builds on the previous ones, and the application will keep growing and getting stronger.

Features Development Roadmap

The landscape of today's web applications is rich with interactive and practical features, many of which users have come to expect as standard. As we move forward, our work will include a broad variety of functionalities that bring modern user experiences to life. The roadmap includes:

- RESTful APIs for the structured management of application data, covering creation, retrieval, updates, and deletion

- Sophisticated pagination and filtering systems that provide users with efficient access to large and complex datasets
- Authentication and authorization mechanisms, including secure user registration, login, role-based access, and two-factor authentication
- Streamlined file upload capabilities, supporting features such as drag-and-drop interfaces, progress tracking, and cloud or local storage
- Background job orchestration for tasks like sending notifications or scheduled reports, ensuring that resource-intensive work never slows down the user experience
- Real-time features that support instant messaging, live notifications, and responsive data updates
- Integrations with popular external services such as social login providers, payment gateways, mapping APIs, and more
- Smart caching and rate limiting to maintain high performance and guard against misuse
- Dynamic document generation, including PDF exports and image processing tailored to specific user needs
- Deployment and operational monitoring tools that automate release workflows and maintain system health
- Comprehensive audit trails and layered security protections that provide accountability and user trust

So, each topic and chapter will naturally build on this foundation, showing you not just how to implement each feature, but also why each step helps you create a maintainable, production-quality application. The method will always be practical and based on real project needs instead of abstract examples.

Why a Unified Stack?

We chose Ubuntu 22.04 LTS as the operating system because it's got a lot of benefits, like long-term support, security, and a really active community. On top of that, Python 3.11 offers better performance, shorter syntax, and access to a bunch of libraries that support what modern developers need. If you pick a unified stack at the start, you can avoid any potential problems or bugs that might come up due to different environments. All the instructions, settings, and methods in this book work with the same platform and requirements, so we'll get consistent results and our code will be easy to move around. We keep our dependency list small, using only a few strong and versatile libraries. This makes things more efficient and reliable. Rather than introducing new packages for every topic, we will make the most of the capabilities of each chosen library. This minimizes installation friction, speeds up onboarding, and makes troubleshooting much easier. If a challenge comes up, we know exactly where to look, and our solution will benefit from strong documentation and widespread industry adoption.

For our project, we will depend on seven libraries, each selected for its versatility and stability:

- ***FastAPI*** stands as the core web framework, enabling us to build RESTful and real-time endpoints efficiently. Its intuitive syntax and automatic documentation features will support every web-facing feature in our project.

- ***Pydantic*** provides robust data validation and configuration management, letting us define clear data models and validate input effortlessly, while also supporting settings management through environment variables.
- ***SQLAlchemy*** (in combination with Alembic) brings ORM power for mapping classes to database tables and handling migrations smoothly, giving us full control over schema evolution and persistence.
- ***Celery*** allows for background task scheduling, batch processing, and handling asynchronous workflows. It enables time-consuming or recurring jobs to run independently, improving performance and user experience.
- ***Redis*** serves a dual purpose, acting both as a high-speed caching layer and as a broker for Celery's messaging. Its ability to handle key-value storage and publish/subscribe patterns makes it invaluable.
- ***Jinja2*** drives our dynamic HTML and PDF generation, providing templating flexibility for front-end components and report exports.
- ***HTTPX*** acts as our HTTP client for all synchronous and asynchronous integrations, supporting everything from third-party API calls to webhook handling.

With these libraries, nearly every feature in modern application development is within reach, from the basics of data handling to advanced integrations and operational monitoring.

Installing Python 3.11

Although Python is often preinstalled, we want to ensure access to the latest Python 3.11 features. The first step involves preparing the package manager and adding a trusted repository:

```
sudo apt update

sudo apt install -y software-properties-common

sudo add-apt-repository ppa:deadsnakes/ppa

sudo apt update

sudo apt install -y python3.11 python3.11-venv python3.11-dev
build-essential
```

These commands achieve several things in a single sweep. First, we update our system to the latest package list, ensuring no surprises during installation. The next line brings in tools that allow us to add new repositories. The deadsnakes PPA offers the most current Python versions for Ubuntu. After updating the package list again, we bring in Python 3.11, its virtual environment module, development headers, and tools for compiling C extensions. At this stage, we are ready to create an isolated Python environment for our project.

Creating Virtual Environment

One of the most important parts of healthy Python development is isolation. We've set up a special virtual environment to keep our global Python installation safe, avoid dependency conflicts, and let each project specify and control its own requirements. The following commands set up this critical workspace in our project directory:

```
python3.11 -m venv .env
```

This creates a directory named **.env**, housing a fresh Python interpreter and a space for dependencies. When we're working on our project, we absolutely have to activate this environment. Here's how you do it:

```
source .env/bin/activate
```

From this point on, any installation or command runs only in this context, shielding our system Python and other projects. Such discipline saves countless hours otherwise spent debugging version mismatches or broken environments. If ever we wish to return to the system shell, a single **deactivate** command brings us back.

Routine Tasks Automation

But as our project grows, the tasks we do become more and more repetitive. From installing dependencies to running tests, maintaining code quality, and starting the development server, these activities are best handled by automation. A Makefile makes our workflow simpler and more consistent.

Following is the Makefile we use to keep things running smoothly:

```
install:
	pip install -r requirements.txt
lint:
	black --check .
	flake8 .
test:
	pytest
dev:
	uvicorn app.main:app --reload
```

The **install** command reads from our **requirements.txt** and ensures all core libraries—FastAPI, Pydantic, SQLAlchemy, Alembic, Celery, Redis, Jinja2, and HTTPX—are present. With **lint**, we verify code style with Black and Flake8, ensuring clean, readable code. The **test** target triggers Pytest for automated checks, and **dev** launches our FastAPI server for live development.

As our project or the app grows, managing its settings and secrets becomes a challenge. By grouping configuration files such as **.env.example**, **alembic.ini**, and **celeryconfig.py** within a dedicated **config/** directory, we maintain clarity and security. This allows us to handle database credentials, secret keys, and migration settings in a centralized and predictable way. When a new configuration variable is required, it will find its place here, so there is never a risk of settings becoming scattered or lost.

CRUD Endpoint Implementation

A robust application begins with a solid foundation for handling its data. Most modern software, from content platforms to e-commerce sites, centers around the ability to create, view, edit, and remove information. These four actions—Create, Read, Update, and Delete—form the backbone of nearly every digital system. Before we can build more advanced features, our first priority is to establish reliable methods for users or systems to interact with data in a structured, predictable, and secure way. Our goal in this topic is to set up our first true set of application features using FastAPI and Pydantic. FastAPI will power our RESTful endpoints, while Pydantic will define and enforce our data schemas.

Sample Data Model

To ground our work in a realistic context, we will start with a simple but universal data model. Suppose we are building a system to manage a collection of books. Each book will have an **id**, a **title**, an **author**, an optional **description**, and a **year** of publication. We are free to expand into more complex objects later, but we keep our first step approachable and directly useful.

Now here, a Pydantic model brings order and type safety to our API. When we define a data model with Pydantic, we describe exactly which fields are required, which are optional, and what types of data are acceptable for each field. This approach prevents bad data from entering our system, and it gives us clear validation errors when something does not match expectations.

The following is how our base model might look, placed in a file such as **app/models.py**:

```
from pydantic import BaseModel, Field
from typing import Optional
class Book(BaseModel):
    id: int
```

```
    title: str = Field(..., min_length=1, max_length=255)
    author: str = Field(..., min_length=1, max_length=100)
    description: Optional[str] = Field(None, max_length=1000)
    year: int = Field(..., ge=1000, le=2100)
```

The use of Pydantic's **`Field`** function allows us to set limits on string lengths and numerical ranges. Required fields use an ellipsis (**`...`**), signaling that they must always be present. There are optional fields, such as **`description`**, that may be omitted or set to **`None`**. If someone tries to submit a book with a missing title or a year outside the accepted range, FastAPI and Pydantic will immediately respond with a helpful validation error.

Designing Service Layer

When you separate the web-facing code from the logic that interacts with data, you've got a clean application. This practice, also known as the "service layer" pattern, has two main advantages: easier testing and better maintainability. Our service layer will handle collecting the books, responding to requests to add, update, retrieve, or delete items.

To show you what I mean, I'll start with an in-memory storage example using a simple Python dictionary. Later on, we'll dive into persistent storage with SQLAlchemy and a real database, but for now, we're keeping it focused on API structure, data validation, and error handling. So now, we will build a basic service for our books in **`app/services.py`**:

```
from app.models import Book
from typing import Dict, List
class BookService:
    def __init__(self):
        self._books: Dict[int, Book] = {}
        self._id_counter: int = 1
    def create_book(self, data: Book) -> Book:
        data.id = self._id_counter
        self._books[self._id_counter] = data
        self._id_counter += 1
        return data
    def get_book(self, book_id: int) -> Book:
        if book_id not in self._books:
```

```
            raise KeyError("Book not found")
        return self._books[book_id]
    def list_books(self) -> List[Book]:
        return list(self._books.values())
    def update_book(self, book_id: int, data: Book) -> Book:
        if book_id not in self._books:
            raise KeyError("Book not found")
        data.id = book_id
        self._books[book_id] = data
        return data
    def delete_book(self, book_id: int) -> None:
        if book_id not in self._books:
            raise KeyError("Book not found")
        del self._books[book_id]
```

This class holds a private dictionary of books, indexed by their IDs. Each new book gets a unique ID, and the class exposes methods for each of the CRUD operations. If a requested book does not exist, the code raises a **KeyError**, which we will handle gracefully in our API layer.

Crafting FastAPI Endpoints

Now, that our data model and service layer in place, we can now expose the CRUD functionality as RESTful endpoints with the help of FastAPI. The each of endpoints will map directly to a common HTTP method:

- ***POST*** for creating new books
- ***GET*** for retrieving a single book or a list of books
- ***PUT*** for updating an existing book
- ***DELETE*** for removing a book

Our API will live in a file named **app/main.py**. To keep things modular, we import our service and models, then define each route clearly and explicitly. We will also use Pydantic's validation to ensure that both requests and responses conform to our expected formats.

The given below is how the FastAPI application will come together:

```
from fastapi import FastAPI, HTTPException
from app.models import Book
```

```
from app.services import BookService
from typing import List
app = FastAPI(title="Book Collection API")
book_service = BookService()
@app.post("/books", response_model=Book, status_code=201)
def create_book(book: Book):
    new_book = book_service.create_book(book)
    return new_book
@app.get("/books/{book_id}", response_model=Book)
def read_book(book_id: int):
    try:
        return book_service.get_book(book_id)
    except KeyError:
        raise HTTPException(status_code=404, detail="Book not
found")
@app.get("/books", response_model=List[Book])
def list_books():
    return book_service.list_books()
@app.put("/books/{book_id}", response_model=Book)
def update_book(book_id: int, book: Book):
    try:
        return book_service.update_book(book_id, book)
    except KeyError:
        raise HTTPException(status_code=404, detail="Book not
found")
@app.delete("/books/{book_id}", status_code=204)
def delete_book(book_id: int):
    try:
        book_service.delete_book(book_id)
    except KeyError:
```

```
        raise HTTPException(status_code=404, detail="Book not
found")
```

In the above, the FastAPI uses function decorators such as **@app.post** and **@app.get** to register endpoints. We also specify the **response_model**, as it guarantees that every successful reply matches the Pydantic schema. And, the HTTP status codes signal to clients whether an operation has succeeded or failed.

Testing CRUD Endpoints

We all know that no feature is complete without a demo that shows it works right. The Swagger UI is auto-generated, so we can test every endpoint with FastAPI's built-in support for interactive documentation. Just go to **http://localhost:8000/docs** after launching the server, we can create books, view lists, retrieve individual items, update information, and delete entries, all without writing any extra code for a testing harness. For example, you might have to create a new book with a valid title and author, then retrieve it by its ID to make sure the data matches. If you try to fetch or update a book with a non-existent ID, you should get a clear 404 error. If you submit a malformed payload, you'll get a 422 error. These examples show that our Pydantic models and error handling are working like they should.

Pagination & Metadata

After building strong CRUD endpoints, we can now handle a lot more realistic data. When we're just starting out, it's easy to forget about the challenge of dealing with hundreds, thousands, or sometimes millions of records for users or client applications. If you don't check it, a basic API endpoint that gets all the books at once can quickly overload the server and client. This wastes bandwidth, slows down the response times, and ultimately makes the experience worse for everyone. This is where thoughtful pagination becomes essential.

A decently designed pagination system does more than split a big set of results into smaller, more manageable pieces. It also introduces a structure that lets users or automated consumers efficiently navigate data, keep their place within long lists, and understand the broader context of their requests. When we build pagination into our API, our users can get exactly what they need, when they need it, without overloading our servers. Plus, a good pagination system should have helpful info like the total number of records and links to each page, so every response is both useful and easy to understand.

Query Parameters

In the earlier CRUD implementation, our **/books** endpoint simply returned all available books. That approach works for small datasets but becomes unmanageable as data grows. To address this, we introduce query parameters—**page** and **page_size**—that control which slice of results should be delivered. And, to keep our logic flexible, we allow sensible defaults, such as the first page and a moderate page size (for example, 10 or 20 items per page). The upper and lower bounds on the page size help us avoid abuse or unintentional overload.

So, the updated endpoint might look like this:

```
from fastapi import Query
@app.get("/books", response_model=List[Book])
def list_books(page: int = Query(1, ge=1), page_size: int =
Query(10, ge=1, le=100)):
    all_books = book_service.list_books()
    start = (page - 1) * page_size
    end = start + page_size
    page_items = all_books[start:end]
    return page_items
```

After doing this, we give every API consumer the power to control their results. The **`Query`** helper from FastAPI enforces default values, as well as minimum and maximum constraints, ensuring a stable experience.

Metadata Headers

For users and automated clients alike, receiving a list of results is only part of the story. Often, knowing how many total records exist, which page is currently shown, and whether more results are available is just as important. This extra information—metadata—enables user interfaces to display page navigation controls, show progress, and support seamless infinite scrolling.

We can enhance our listing endpoint to include custom HTTP headers in each response. These headers communicate the total number of records, the current page, the total number of pages, and URLs for the next and previous pages when available.

So now, to achieve this, we adjust our endpoint as follows:

```
from fastapi import Response
@app.get("/books", response_model=List[Book])
def list_books(
    page: int = Query(1, ge=1),
    page_size: int = Query(10, ge=1, le=100),
    response: Response = None
```

```
):
    all_books = book_service.list_books()
    total = len(all_books)
    start = (page - 1) * page_size
    end = start + page_size
    page_items = all_books[start:end]
    total_pages = (total + page_size - 1) // page_size
    response.headers["X-Total-Count"] = str(total)
    response.headers["X-Current-Page"] = str(page)
    response.headers["X-Page-Size"] = str(page_size)
    response.headers["X-Total-Pages"] = str(total_pages)
    if page < total_pages:
        response.headers["X-Next-Page"] =
f"/books?page={page+1}&page_size={page_size}"
    if page > 1:
        response.headers["X-Previous-Page"] =
f"/books?page={page-1}&page_size={page_size}"
    return page_items
```

Now that we've got these headers, our API's got everything a client needs to build a sophisticated, interactive experience. They can easily show pagination controls, the total result count, and navigation links.

Cursor-Based Pagination

The offset-based pagination method, which uses **page** and **page_size**, works well for small or moderately-sized datasets. But as collections grow, this method can have accuracy and performance issues, especially when records are added or removed between requests. Cursor-based pagination solves a lot of these problems by providing a marker, or "cursor," that precisely identifies the last record seen in the previous response. Then, the next page is fetched using this cursor, which can be an ID, a timestamp, or any unique field.

To make cursor-based pagination work, we just modify our service layer to accept a cursor parameter. When the client provides a cursor, we fetch the next set of results starting after the specified record. To show you what I mean, we'll use the book's **ID** field as our cursor:

```
from typing import Optional
@app.get("/books-cursor", response_model=List[Book])
def list_books_cursor(
    cursor: Optional[int] = Query(None),
    page_size: int = Query(10, ge=1, le=100),
    response: Response = None
):
    all_books = sorted(book_service.list_books(), key=lambda
b: b.id)
    if cursor is not None:
        filtered_books = [book for book in all_books if
book.id > cursor]
    else:
        filtered_books = all_books
    page_items = filtered_books[:page_size]
    if page_items:
        response.headers["X-Next-Cursor"] = str(page_items[-
1].id)
    return page_items
```

After this, the clients can now keep track of the last **`id`** they received and use it as the **`cursor`** value for the next request. It is particularly well-suited for applications with continuously updating data, such as chat messages or transaction logs.

Metadata for Cursor Pagination

And when it comes to navigating with a cursor, metadata is key for helping clients manage their navigation state. If we return the next cursor value in the response headers, the client can seamlessly request the next set of results. If no more results are available, the absence of a **`X-Next-Cursor`** header signals the end of the dataset. The same pattern can be extended to support both previous and next cursors, making bi-directional navigation possible if required. This level of flexibility allows our API to support a wide range of user experiences, from simple pagination controls to real-time, infinite scrolling interfaces.

Handling Synchronous and Asynchronous Database Calls

We've been using in-memory storage so far, which runs in the main server thread. But in the real world, we use persistent databases, which are often accessed asynchronously to make sure everything runs smoothly when there's a lot of traffic. FastAPI makes it a breeze to support both synchronous and asynchronous endpoints.

For synchronous access, our service functions perform direct database queries and return results right away. When we're working with an asynchronous database driver, like the ones used with PostgreSQL or MongoDB, we define our endpoints with the **async def** syntax and use **await** to fetch results. FastAPI automatically manages the execution context, ensuring that concurrent requests are handled efficiently.

Following is a quick example of an asynchronous endpoint for listing books might look like this:

```
@app.get("/books-async", response_model=List[Book])
async def list_books_async(
    page: int = Query(1, ge=1),
    page_size: int = Query(10, ge=1, le=100),
    response: Response = None
):
    all_books = await async_book_service.list_books()
    total = len(all_books)
    start = (page - 1) * page_size
    end = start + page_size
    page_items = all_books[start:end]
    response.headers["X-Total-Count"] = str(total)
    return page_items
```

With this system, we can easily switch between synchronous and asynchronous calls, which lets us handle more traffic. The service layer can support both styles, and our endpoints only require small changes to adapt. The move from simple in-memory management to solid, database-backed storage is a huge step for our project. We've done a lot of work to set up our endpoints, check the data, and show the results with pagination and metadata. This makes it so we're all set to move forward.

Advanced Filtering & Sorting

Up to this point, we have focused on serving manageable slices of data, with clear pagination and essential metadata guiding each API response. While these tools already provide a major upgrade over simple data dumps, real-world applications frequently demand even more precision and flexibility. In any serious product, users want to search, filter, and order data based on their exact needs, perhaps narrowing a list of books to a certain author, searching within a publication range, or sorting results by the newest or most popular titles.

To deliver this level of control, our endpoints must grow more dynamic. Instead of returning all books in a fixed order, we empower clients to specify filters across multiple fields and request results in their preferred order. The challenge is to support these flexible queries without cluttering our code with endless conditional branches. With the power of SQLAlchemy, we can achieve this goal by adapting database queries at runtime, responding gracefully to whatever combination of filters and sort orders the user provides.

Parsing Complex Query Parameters

Modern APIs commonly allow clients to filter by any combination of available fields. For our books example, users might want to retrieve only titles by a specific author, select books published after a certain year, or even combine several conditions at once. The FastAPI makes this straightforward by exposing query parameters directly in our endpoint functions. We can accept optional parameters such as **author**, **year_min**, and **year_max**, and then dynamically build the filtering logic based on which ones are present in the request. Pydantic also plays a role here, helping us validate and parse the types of each filter.

Given below is a simple code structure for our enhanced filtering endpoint:

```
from typing import Optional, List
from fastapi import Query
@app.get("/books/search", response_model=List[Book])
def search_books(
    author: Optional[str] = Query(None, min_length=1,
max_length=100),
    year_min: Optional[int] = Query(None, ge=1000, le=2100),
    year_max: Optional[int] = Query(None, ge=1000, le=2100),
    title: Optional[str] = Query(None, min_length=1,
max_length=255)
):
    query = db.query(BookModel)
    if author:
```

```
        query =
query.filter(BookModel.author.ilike(f"%{author}%"))
    if year_min:
        query = query.filter(BookModel.year >= year_min)
    if year_max:
        query = query.filter(BookModel.year <= year_max)
    if title:
        query =
query.filter(BookModel.title.ilike(f"%{title}%"))
    results = query.all()
    return [Book.from_orm(b) for b in results]
```

This pattern accepts any or all filters in a single call. The code adapts its query depending on the presence of each parameter, skipping unnecessary conditions while always returning correct results.

Multi-Field Sorting with Dynamic Directions

While filtering makes things more precise, users also want the ability to order their results. Whether they want to see the most recent entries first, sort alphabetically by title, or highlight certain authors, robust sorting is a must-have. To support this, we're introducing two new query parameters: **sort_by** and **sort_dir**. The first allows clients to specify which field should control the order (such as **year**, **title**, or **author**), while the second sets the direction, either ascending or descending.

Once again, the endpoint code adapts at runtime. SQLAlchemy's ordering functions make it possible to build the **ORDER BY** clause dynamically, based on safe, validated inputs from the client.

The given below is how our enhanced endpoint might look:

```
from sqlalchemy import asc, desc
@app.get("/books/search", response_model=List[Book])
def search_books(
    author: Optional[str] = Query(None, min_length=1,
max_length=100),
    year_min: Optional[int] = Query(None, ge=1000, le=2100),
    year_max: Optional[int] = Query(None, ge=1000, le=2100),
```

```
    title: Optional[str] = Query(None, min_length=1,
max_length=255),
    sort_by: Optional[str] = Query("year"),
    sort_dir: Optional[str] = Query("desc")
):
    sort_column = getattr(BookModel, sort_by, None)
    if not sort_column:
        sort_column = BookModel.year
    direction = desc if sort_dir.lower() == "desc" else asc
    query = db.query(BookModel)
    if author:
        query =
query.filter(BookModel.author.ilike(f"%{author}%"))
    if year_min:
        query = query.filter(BookModel.year >= year_min)
    if year_max:
        query = query.filter(BookModel.year <= year_max)
    if title:
        query =
query.filter(BookModel.title.ilike(f"%{title}%"))
    query = query.order_by(direction(sort_column))
    results = query.all()
    return [Book.from_orm(b) for b in results]
```

After this, the users gain full control over both which records appear and the order in which they arrive. The logic automatically rejects unknown fields and defaults to a safe, predictable order.

Combining Conditions for Powerful Search Patterns

In many use cases, filtering and sorting operate together. For example, a user might want to see all books by a certain author, published after a specific year, sorted by title in ascending order. With the buildup of our queries as a chain of conditional filters and a final dynamic sort, we keep the code flexible and performant. Each new filter simply appends another condition to the SQLAlchemy query, without duplicating logic. Because the code adapts at runtime, we avoid a tangle of nested if-else blocks. Every optional filter stands alone, and adding new fields in the future becomes trivial. The SQL generated by SQLAlchemy always reflects only the necessary conditions—ensuring fast queries and clear, maintainable code.

When new requirements appear, such as adding search by genre or language, the same pattern supports rapid expansion. Our API stays lean while growing more useful with each enhancement.

Handling Synchronous and Asynchronous Filtering

SQLAlchemy supports both synchronous and asynchronous database access, and FastAPI makes it possible to write endpoints for each style. In high-traffic applications, asynchronous queries often deliver better scalability and responsiveness. By creating both versions of our endpoints, we equip our application to handle present and future needs.

For a synchronous pattern, the code uses direct queries and immediate results. When working asynchronously, we write our endpoint as **`async def`**, leverage async database sessions, and use **`await`** for all query operations. This makes our backend truly modern, ready for real-world load and concurrency.

A simple asynchronous version of our filtering endpoint would look like this:

```
@app.get("/books/search-async", response_model=List[Book])
async def search_books_async(
    author: Optional[str] = Query(None, min_length=1,
max_length=100),
    year_min: Optional[int] = Query(None, ge=1000, le=2100),
    year_max: Optional[int] = Query(None, ge=1000, le=2100),
    title: Optional[str] = Query(None, min_length=1,
max_length=255),
    sort_by: Optional[str] = Query("year"),
    sort_dir: Optional[str] = Query("desc")
):
    # Build dynamic SQLAlchemy query here, using async session
and await
    # Example only: implementation details will depend on
chosen async database library
    pass
```

By offering both access patterns, our API stands ready for high-performance applications and large datasets.

Next, we'll connect these dynamic endpoints to solid import and export abilities. That way, whether it's handling user-driven queries or moving bulk data around, our app will stay agile and scalable.

Bulk Import/Export

With a solid foundation of CRUD operations, advanced filtering, and flexible sorting, our app now delivers an interactive and highly usable API for users and client systems. But being able to move a lot of data into and out of our system is essential. Whether it's onboarding new customers with thousands of records, performing migrations from legacy systems, or enabling business users to extract actionable insights, bulk import and export operations become the gateway for efficient data exchange. When it comes to handling large amounts of data, there's more to consider than just making sure it's correct. An import process has to make sure it's all good and legit, so it's got to accept only valid and complete data, report any errors openly, and avoid doing updates that are only partly there or don't line up. Export operations also need to deliver reliable, well-formatted outputs, often as CSV or JSON streams, to be used as inputs for analytics pipelines, third-party integrations, or simple reporting. Since these datasets can grow by the thousands or millions, we've got to make sure our design doesn't end up throwing off our memory or performance. As we work on these tools together, streaming, batching, and incremental processing will be essential techniques.

Designing Export Utilities

The challenge of exporting data at scale lies in maintaining performance and avoiding resource exhaustion. Rather than constructing a giant list or string of all records, we employ streaming—a pattern where each record is written to the output as it is processed, and only a small portion of data ever occupies memory. The FastAPI provides powerful support for streaming responses. For CSV exports, we leverage Python's standard **csv** module and yield lines directly as the response is being sent. For JSON, a similar streaming technique is used, yielding one object at a time in a properly formatted sequence.

The given below is how a streaming CSV export might look:

```
from fastapi.responses import StreamingResponse
import csv
from io import StringIO
@app.get("/books/export/csv")
def export_books_csv():
    def generate():
```

```
        output = StringIO()
        writer = csv.writer(output)
        writer.writerow(['id', 'title', 'author',
'description', 'year'])
        yield output.getvalue()
        output.seek(0)
        output.truncate(0)
        for book in book_service.list_books():
            writer.writerow([book.id, book.title, book.author,
book.description, book.year])
            yield output.getvalue()
            output.seek(0)
            output.truncate(0)
    return StreamingResponse(generate(),
media_type="text/csv", headers={
        "Content-Disposition": "attachment;
filename=books.csv"
    })
```

This method writes the header row first, then yields each book record as it is processed. At no point does the entire data set need to reside in memory. Even if our book collection grows to a million records, the export remains fast and reliable.

The streaming of JSON responses also follows a similar philosophy. While JSON arrays must be wrapped with opening and closing brackets, each item can still be yielded individually. This streaming approach can support real-time dashboards, long-running exports, or integration with downstream analytics systems.

Implementing Streaming JSON Export

One more thing to watch out for when streaming JSON in an HTTP response is... You need to use a comma between objects in a JSON array, but not before the first or after the last. The FastAPI's **StreamingResponse** and careful iterator logic allow us to deliver standards-compliant output. Each book object is converted to a dictionary and serialized on the fly.

Following is a simple way of exporting all books as a streaming JSON array:

```
import json
```

```
@app.get("/books/export/json")
def export_books_json():
    def generate():
        yield '['
        first = True
        for book in book_service.list_books():
            if not first:
                yield ','
            yield json.dumps(book.dict())
            first = False
        yield ']'
    return StreamingResponse(generate(),
media_type="application/json", headers={
        "Content-Disposition": "attachment;
filename=books.json"
    })
```

The clients receive the array as it is constructed, and memory use remains low regardless of dataset size. This streaming pattern is a vital building block for high-volume, production-ready data pipelines.

Creating Bulk Import Utilities

The bulk imports introduce both opportunities and risks. When performed carelessly, they can admit corrupt, incomplete, or malicious data into the system. Our import utilities must be vigilant—validating every record, rejecting incomplete or invalid entries, and providing detailed feedback for each error encountered.

For CSV imports, FastAPI's file upload support and Python's **csv** module make it straightforward to process rows one by one. Validation occurs on each line, and only records that pass all checks are inserted or updated in the application's core storage. JSON imports follow a similar approach but can support more complex, nested objects.

Following is a template for streaming, validating, and importing CSV data:

```
from fastapi import File, UploadFile
import csv
```

```
from io import StringIO
@app.post("/books/import/csv")
async def import_books_csv(file: UploadFile = File(...)):
    content = await file.read()
    file_stream = StringIO(content.decode())
    reader = csv.DictReader(file_stream)
    results = {"created": 0, "failed": 0, "errors": []}
    for idx, row in enumerate(reader, start=1):
        try:
            book = Book(
                id=0,  # ID will be assigned by the service
                title=row["title"],
                author=row["author"],
                description=row.get("description"),
                year=int(row["year"])
            )
            book_service.create_book(book)
            results["created"] += 1
        except Exception as e:
            results["failed"] += 1
            results["errors"].append({"row": idx, "error":
str(e)})
    return results
```

in the above, each row is read and validated as a potential book record. If a field is missing or the data does not conform to the Pydantic schema, an error is recorded. At the end, a summary is returned, indicating how many records succeeded, how many failed, and providing a detailed list of errors by row number. The JSON imports also work similarly, with each object in the input array undergoing the same rigorous validation before becoming part of our application's dataset.

So now, with the robust bulk import and export utilities now in place, our application stands ready for real-world, production-grade data movement. The clients can retrieve vast datasets, perform detailed analytics, or onboard and synchronize thousands of records with minimal friction and maximum safety. These capabilities form the gateway for enterprise-scale usage, migrations, integrations, and more. In the next chapter, we will build on this strong data foundation by introducing authentication and authorization mechanisms. These additions will empower us to control access, enforce permissions, and secure all the data management features we have built so far. Every enhancement remains deeply connected to our central objectives: practical, scalable, and reliable software, developed step by step in a single, cohesive project.

Summary

In all, we got a solid Python development environment up and running, and a virtual environment to keep things separate. We set up the project structure and the main library, making sure that every next feature could be developed on a predictable and consistent foundation. We built our first data model and created service patterns to handle books, then developed RESTful CRUD endpoints using FastAPI and Pydantic, enforcing strong request and response validation. We made sure to include error handling at each step, so our API is both robust and user-friendly. We were able to efficiently handle large amounts of data thanks to improvements in pagination and metadata. And with cursor-based navigation, our endpoints had the scalability needed for actual apps. We advanced to implementing multi-field filtering and dynamic sorting, constructing flexible queries with SQLAlchemy that adapted to any combination of client parameters.

We finally added some bulk import and export utilities. They support both CSV and JSON formats and use streaming techniques to make sure our data moves reliably and safely. At every step, we focused on building code that's easy to maintain, protecting data integrity, and setting patterns that could be extended in all future chapters.

CHAPTER 2: AUTHENTICATION & AUTHORIZATION

Overview

This chapter is all about how to design and set up a modern authentication and authorization system for our Python applications. We'll start by going over the basics of setting up secure user registration. This means using time-limited email confirmation tokens and asynchronous delivery to make sure that only real users end up activating their accounts. You'll learn how to hash and validate credentials with bcrypt, and then move on to creating a login process that uses JWTs or session cookies for smooth authentication.

This chapter will walk you through building a reliable password reset flow, so users can safely recover their accounts using secure, expiring tokens. As we go through this, you'll learn the ropes of role-based access control, how to define permissions, map them to user roles, and enforce rules across our API endpoints. The final part will teach you about two-factor authentication using TOTP, including generating shared secrets and QR code provisioning and making second-factor checks. You'll also learn how to apply lockout policies to prevent repeated failed attempts. Once you get through these topics, you'll be able to deliver solid, flexible, and easy-to-use security for any web application with a lot of features.

User Registration & Email Confirmation

Designing User Model

Before we do anything else, we need a way to represent users in our app. We must learn to store an email, a password (hashed), and track whether a user has activated their account. So, to do this, in our **models.py**, we define both a Pydantic schema for user creation and a SQLAlchemy model for the database:

```
from pydantic import BaseModel, EmailStr, Field
from typing import Optional
from sqlalchemy import Column, Integer, String, Boolean,
DateTime
from sqlalchemy.ext.declarative import declarative_base
from datetime import datetime
Base = declarative_base()
class UserCreate(BaseModel):
    email: EmailStr
    password: str = Field(..., min_length=8, max_length=128)
```

```
class UserOut(BaseModel):
    id: int
    email: EmailStr
    is_active: bool
class UserModel(Base):
    __tablename__ = "users"
    id = Column(Integer, primary_key=True, index=True)
    email = Column(String, unique=True, index=True,
nullable=False)
    hashed_password = Column(String, nullable=False)
    is_active = Column(Boolean, default=False)
    created_at = Column(DateTime, default=datetime.utcnow)
```

This model ensures every account is inactive until the owner confirms their email.

Creating Secure Password Hash

We should never store plain passwords. To make sure our database is safe even in the event of a leak, we hash every password with bcrypt using the **passlib** library. So to do this, in our **security.py**, we add the following helper:

```
from passlib.context import CryptContext
pwd_context = CryptContext(schemes=["bcrypt"],
deprecated="auto")
def hash_password(password: str) -> str:
    return pwd_context.hash(password)
```

This function will always be used before a password touches the database.

Building User Registration Endpoint

Now here, our registration API needs to handle several things:

- Accepting a user's email and password
- Checking for duplicate emails
- Hashing the password
- Creating a new, inactive user
- Triggering a confirmation email in the background

We implement all of this in the **routes/auth.py**:

```
from fastapi import APIRouter, HTTPException, status, 
BackgroundTasks, Depends
from sqlalchemy.orm import Session
from app.models import UserCreate, UserModel
from app.security import hash_password
from app.db import get_db
router = APIRouter()
@router.post("/register", status_code=status.HTTP_201_CREATED)
def register(user: UserCreate, background_tasks: 
BackgroundTasks, db: Session = Depends(get_db)):
    if db.query(UserModel).filter(UserModel.email == 
user.email).first():
        raise HTTPException(status_code=400, detail="Email 
already registered")
    hashed_pw = hash_password(user.password)
    new_user = UserModel(email=user.email, 
hashed_password=hashed_pw, is_active=False)
    db.add(new_user)
    db.commit()
    db.refresh(new_user)
    from app.email import send_confirmation_email
    background_tasks.add_task(send_confirmation_email, 
new_user.email, new_user.id)
    return {"msg": "Registration successful. Please check our 
email to confirm our account."}
```

With this endpoint, every new user starts inactive, and a confirmation email is queued immediately after registration.

Generating Time-Limited Confirmation Token

Next, a token is needed for every signup so only the real email owner can activate the account. In **tokens.py**, we create helpers using **itsdangerous** that allow us to generate and later verify a time-limited token tied to the user's ID.

```
from itsdangerous import URLSafeTimedSerializer
SECRET_KEY = "super-secret"  # In production, load from
config!
CONFIRM_SALT = "email-confirm"
def generate_confirmation_token(user_id: int):
    s = URLSafeTimedSerializer(SECRET_KEY)
    return s.dumps(user_id, salt=CONFIRM_SALT)
def verify_confirmation_token(token: str, expiration=1800):
    s = URLSafeTimedSerializer(SECRET_KEY)
    try:
        return s.loads(token, salt=CONFIRM_SALT,
max_age=expiration)
    except Exception:
        return None
```

Every confirmation link uses this token, and it remains valid for 30 minutes by default.

Sending Confirmation Email

To avoid slowing down registration, we send the email in the background. Our initial setup uses FastAPI's **BackgroundTasks** for simplicity; moving to Celery later is easy. In **email.py**, we define the function:

```
from app.tokens import generate_confirmation_token
def send_confirmation_email(email: str, user_id: int):
    token = generate_confirmation_token(user_id)
    confirm_url =
f"http://localhost:8000/verify?token={token}"
    subject = "Confirm our account"
    body = f"Hi,\n\nPlease confirm our account by clicking the
link below:\n{confirm_url}\n\nThis link expires in 30
minutes."
```

```
    # In production, use an email backend (e.g., smtplib,
SendGrid)
    print(f"Send to {email}: {body}")
```

With this, every registration triggers an email containing a secure confirmation link.

Verifying User Accounts

When a user clicks the confirmation link in their email, they reach the **/verify** endpoint. Here, we take care of validating the token, checking if there's already a user with the same email, and, if it's good to go, we'll activate their account. If there's an error, like an expired token, invalid user, or something's already active, it'll be handled smoothly.

```
from app.tokens import verify_confirmation_token
@router.get("/verify")
def verify_email(token: str, db: Session = Depends(get_db)):
    user_id = verify_confirmation_token(token)
    if not user_id:
        raise HTTPException(status_code=400, detail="Invalid
or expired token")
    user = db.query(UserModel).filter(UserModel.id ==
user_id).first()
    if not user:
        raise HTTPException(status_code=404, detail="User not
found")
    if user.is_active:
        return {"msg": "Account already activated"}
    user.is_active = True
    db.commit()
    return {"msg": "Email confirmed. You may now log in."}
```

With all these steps in place, our registration process now works as follows:

1. A user submits their email and password to **/register**.
2. The password is hashed and saved.
3. The account is marked inactive, and a background task sends an email with a confirmation link.

4. The user receives the email, clicks the link, and the **/verify** endpoint checks the token.
5. If everything checks out, the account becomes active and ready for login.

For projects with high traffic, the FastAPI's **BackgroundTasks** may eventually be replaced with Celery, letting us handle email delivery in a distributed, reliable way. The code for Celery integration is almost identical. We simply point the background task at a Celery worker, and all confirmation emails are handled outside the API server, ensuring smooth performance even under load.

Secure Login & Password Reset

Introducing 'bcrypt'

We already store passwords as bcrypt hashes, but before any login or password reset is possible, we will revisit why bcrypt matters. Plain passwords are a critical risk; a hash protects the data, even if the database leaks. bcrypt, in particular, is built to slow down brute-force attacks, making it the default for nearly every secure Python project.

In our **security.py**, we have already added the password hashing function using **passlib**:

```
from passlib.context import CryptContext
pwd_context = CryptContext(schemes=["bcrypt"],
deprecated="auto")
def hash_password(password: str) -> str:
    return pwd_context.hash(password)
def verify_password(plain: str, hashed: str) -> bool:
    return pwd_context.verify(plain, hashed)
```

The **verify_password** function will be called every time a user tries to log in, comparing the password they typed to the hash in our database.

Secure Login Endpoint

Now, we're working on a system that'll let users log in with just their email and password. We'll look up the user, check their status, and use bcrypt to verify their password. If it's successful, we'll give you a JWT (JSON Web Token) so you can confirm future requests. So here, we will now define a Pydantic schema for login data, then create a login route in **routes/auth.py**:

```
from pydantic import BaseModel, EmailStr
class LoginRequest(BaseModel):
```

```
    email: EmailStr
    password: str
```

In our route, we add the login logic:

```
from fastapi import APIRouter, HTTPException, status, Depends
from sqlalchemy.orm import Session
from app.models import UserModel
from app.security import verify_password
from app.tokens import create_jwt_token  # Will define below
from app.db import get_db
router = APIRouter()
@router.post("/login")
def login(data: LoginRequest, db: Session = Depends(get_db)):
    user = db.query(UserModel).filter(UserModel.email ==
data.email).first()
    if not user or not user.is_active:
        raise HTTPException(status_code=401, detail="Invalid
credentials or inactive account")
    if not verify_password(data.password,
user.hashed_password):
        raise HTTPException(status_code=401, detail="Invalid
credentials or inactive account")
    token = create_jwt_token(user.id, user.email)
    return {"access_token": token, "token_type": "bearer"}
```

This endpoint accepts the credentials, checks everything, and issues an access token only if all is well. The token lets the user access protected APIs.

Generating JWT Access Tokens

A JWT is a signed token that encodes identity and expiration, passed by the client on every request. Inside **tokens.py**, we define helpers for creating and decoding JWTs:

```
import jwt
```

```
from datetime import datetime, timedelta
JWT_SECRET = "jwt-secret-key"  # Move to config in production!
JWT_ALGORITHM = "HS256"
JWT_EXPIRE_MINUTES = 30
def create_jwt_token(user_id: int, email: str):
    payload = {
        "sub": str(user_id),
        "email": email,
        "exp": datetime.utcnow() +
timedelta(minutes=JWT_EXPIRE_MINUTES),
    }
    return jwt.encode(payload, JWT_SECRET,
algorithm=JWT_ALGORITHM)
def decode_jwt_token(token: str):
    try:
        return jwt.decode(token, JWT_SECRET,
algorithms=[JWT_ALGORITHM])
    except jwt.ExpiredSignatureError:
        return None
    except jwt.InvalidTokenError:
        return None
```

When a user logs in, the server gives them a token containing their ID, email, and an expiry timestamp. Every protected endpoint will check the validity of this token.

Authenticating Protected Endpoints

To check user identity on protected APIs, we add a dependency that extracts the JWT from the Authorization header, decodes it, and retrieves the current user. We use FastAPI's dependency injection:

```
from fastapi import Depends, HTTPException, status
from fastapi.security import OAuth2PasswordBearer
from sqlalchemy.orm import Session
```

```
from app.tokens import decode_jwt_token
from app.models import UserModel
from app.db import get_db
oauth2_scheme = OAuth2PasswordBearer(tokenUrl="login")
def get_current_user(token: str = Depends(oauth2_scheme), db: Session = Depends(get_db)):
    payload = decode_jwt_token(token)
    if not payload:
        raise HTTPException(status_code=401, detail="Invalid or expired token")
    user = db.query(UserModel).filter(UserModel.id == int(payload["sub"])).first()
    if not user:
        raise HTTPException(status_code=404, detail="User not found")
    return user
```

Every secure endpoint now simply includes **`current_user: UserModel = Depends(get_current_user)`**, and unauthorized access is blocked.

Implementing Password Reset

A secure app allows users to reset forgotten passwords. The process involves two main endpoints:

1. ***Request password reset***: User enters their email, and the server emails them a secure, time-bound token.
2. ***Confirm password reset***: User clicks the link, provides a new password, and the server validates the token before updating credentials.

Here, at first, we define the schema for requesting a reset:

```
from pydantic import BaseModel, EmailStr
class PasswordResetRequest(BaseModel):
    email: EmailStr
```

Now, in **`routes/auth.py`**, we then add the reset request endpoint:

```
from app.email import send_password_reset_email
```

```
@router.post("/password-reset/request")
def password_reset_request(data: PasswordResetRequest, db:
Session = Depends(get_db)):
    user = db.query(UserModel).filter(UserModel.email ==
data.email).first()
    if not user or not user.is_active:
        # Do not reveal which emails are registered for
privacy
        return {"msg": "If that email is registered, a reset
link has been sent."}
    from app.tokens import generate_password_reset_token
    token = generate_password_reset_token(user.id)
    send_password_reset_email(user.email, token)
    return {"msg": "If that email is registered, a reset link
has been sent."}
```

This will keep the response generic and protects privacy. Next, we then define the token generator in **`tokens.py`** (similar to our confirmation token):

```
def generate_password_reset_token(user_id: int):
    s = URLSafeTimedSerializer(SECRET_KEY)
    return s.dumps(user_id, salt="password-reset")
def verify_password_reset_token(token: str, expiration=1800):
    s = URLSafeTimedSerializer(SECRET_KEY)
    try:
        return s.loads(token, salt="password-reset",
max_age=expiration)
    except Exception:
        return None
```

The email function builds the reset URL and sends the token:

```
def send_password_reset_email(email: str, token: str):
```

```
    reset_url = f"http://localhost:8000/password-
reset/confirm?token={token}"
    body = f"Click to reset our password: {reset_url}\nThis
link expires in 30 minutes."
    print(f"Send to {email}: {body}")
```

Completing Password Reset

When the user clicks the reset link, they land on the frontend, which will submit their new password and token to an endpoint like **/password-reset/confirm**. So here, we will now define a schema and the endpoint:

```
class PasswordResetConfirm(BaseModel):
    token: str
    new_password: str = Field(..., min_length=8,
max_length=128)
```

Add the confirmation endpoint:

```
@router.post("/password-reset/confirm")
def password_reset_confirm(data: PasswordResetConfirm, db:
Session = Depends(get_db)):
    from app.tokens import verify_password_reset_token
    user_id = verify_password_reset_token(data.token)
    if not user_id:
        raise HTTPException(status_code=400, detail="Invalid
or expired token")
    user = db.query(UserModel).filter(UserModel.id ==
user_id).first()
    if not user:
        raise HTTPException(status_code=404, detail="User not
found")
    user.hashed_password = hash_password(data.new_password)
    db.commit()
    return {"msg": "Password has been reset successfully."}
```

No password ever travels or is stored in plain text. The token ensures only the user with access to their email can change the credentials, and all tokens are single-use and expire after a set time.

To quickly review our login and password reset flow, see the following:

- Users log in with bcrypt-protected credentials.
- On login, a JWT is issued, allowing stateless, secure access to protected APIs.
- Password resets are handled by a time-limited token emailed only to verified users.
- The reset process never leaks registration status, guards against token abuse, and ensures only the account owner can update credentials.

The next natural topic is role-based access and fine-grained permission enforcement, which will grow directly from the authentication foundation established here.

Role-Based Access Control

Role-Based Access Control, or RBAC, gives us a flexible, scalable way to manage permissions. We can assign capabilities to roles, and roles to users. This helps us avoid having to hard-code access rules everywhere. It's better than ad hoc checks or a simple "is_admin" flag because it lets us support teams, customer tiers, moderators, and evolving requirements without rewriting business logic. It also makes audits and compliance easier, since every action is tied to a specific role and permission. The RBAC is different from other options like Access Control Lists (ACLs) and Attribute-Based Access Control (ABAC). ACLs can get unwieldy as systems grow, and ABAC's flexibility comes with a trade-off: increased complexity. It's a pretty balanced system, you can grant or revoke power by changing a user's role, and the rules for permission are all defined in one place.

Modeling Roles and Permissions

Our first step is to represent roles and map permissions in our codebase. To do this, we will update our user model in **`models.py`** so each user has a **`role`**. In the simplest form, we can use a string field for role and a Python dictionary to define permissions for each role:

```
# app/models.py
from sqlalchemy import Column, String
# ... other imports and UserModel definition ...
class UserModel(Base):
    __tablename__ = "users"
    id = Column(Integer, primary_key=True, index=True)
    email = Column(String, unique=True, index=True,
nullable=False)
```

```
    hashed_password = Column(String, nullable=False)
    is_active = Column(Boolean, default=False)
    role = Column(String, default="user")
    created_at = Column(DateTime, default=datetime.utcnow)
```

We then define the permission rules in a central place **permissions.py** using a dictionary where each role maps to a set of allowed actions:

```
# app/permissions.py
PERMISSIONS = {
    "user": {"read_profile", "update_profile"},
    "moderator": {"read_profile", "update_profile",
"ban_user"},
    "admin": {"read_profile", "update_profile", "ban_user",
"manage_roles", "delete_user"}
}
```

This allows you to add, remove, or rename permissions for any role without touching the routes.

Creating Permission Decorator

Now if we want to enforce RBAC, we'll need a decorator that checks whether the current user has the required permission before running any route logic. For this, we will add this to **permissions.py**:

```
from fastapi import Depends, HTTPException, status
from functools import wraps
from app.routes.auth import get_current_user  # Already
defined in previous topics
def require_permission(permission: str):
    def decorator(func):
        @wraps(func)
        def wrapper(*args, **kwargs):
            current_user = kwargs.get('current_user')
            if not current_user:
```

```
                # In FastAPI, this will be injected via
dependency
                raise HTTPException(status_code=401,
detail="Authentication required")
            role = getattr(current_user, "role", "user")
            allowed = PERMISSIONS.get(role, set())
            if permission not in allowed:
                raise HTTPException(status_code=403,
detail="Permission denied")
            return func(*args, **kwargs)
        return wrapper
    return decorator
```

Alternatively, for FastAPI, we can use a dependency-based approach, which is more idiomatic, and here is how you can write it:

```
def permission_required(permission: str):
    def dependency(current_user = Depends(get_current_user)):
        role = getattr(current_user, "role", "user")
        allowed = PERMISSIONS.get(role, set())
        if permission not in allowed:
            raise HTTPException(status_code=403,
detail="Permission denied")
        return True
    return Depends(dependency)
```

This allows us to enforce permissions in route dependencies.

Applying RBAC to API Routes

Okay, next up we're going to lock down some endpoints using our RBAC logic. For example, imagine a route where only admins can delete users, and only moderators or admins can ban users. Here's an example of how you could use it:

```
from fastapi import APIRouter, Depends
from app.permissions import permission_required
```

```
router = APIRouter()
@router.delete("/users/{user_id}")
def delete_user(user_id: int,
                current_user = Depends(get_current_user),
                perm = permission_required("delete_user")):
    # Service logic here
    # Only admins will reach this point
    # ...
    return {"msg": f"User {user_id} deleted"}
@router.post("/users/{user_id}/ban")
def ban_user(user_id: int,
             current_user = Depends(get_current_user),
             perm = permission_required("ban_user")):
    # Only moderators or admins will reach here
    # ...
    return {"msg": f"User {user_id} banned"}
```

The FastAPI ensures the user is authenticated and the permission check passes before calling our business logic. If a user without the proper role tries to access a protected route, they receive a 403 error.

Enforcing RBAC

The middleware can also be used to enforce RBAC at a broader level—checking permissions globally or logging unauthorized attempts for audits. For most projects, the dependency/decorator pattern above is flexible enough, but for cross-cutting concerns (such as logging, usage analytics, or centralized denial responses), adding a custom middleware is a natural next step in my opinion.

So here is a simple way to enforce middleware-based RBAC:

```
from fastapi import Request
from starlette.middleware.base import BaseHTTPMiddleware
class RBACMiddleware(BaseHTTPMiddleware):
    async def dispatch(self, request: Request, call_next):
```

```
        # Example: log or enforce RBAC globally
        # You can access user, path, etc. here
        response = await call_next(request)
        return response
```

You can plug this into our app for monitoring or system-wide policy enforcement.

Managing Roles and Permissions Dynamically

In some applications, roles or permissions may change over time, like the admins promote or demote users, or new roles are added. This can be managed by updating the user's **role** field in the database and maintaining a clear, version-controlled **PERMISSIONS** dictionary. For more dynamic needs, roles and permissions could also be modeled as database tables, allowing for runtime updates without code changes.

To modify a user's role, an admin can hit a protected endpoint:

```
@router.patch("/users/{user_id}/role")
def update_role(user_id: int, new_role: str,
                current_user = Depends(get_current_user),
                perm = permission_required("manage_roles"),
                db: Session = Depends(get_db)):
    user = db.query(UserModel).filter(UserModel.id ==
user_id).first()
    if not user:
        raise HTTPException(status_code=404, detail="User not
found")
    user.role = new_role
    db.commit()
    return {"msg": f"Role updated to {new_role}"}
```

With these patterns in place, you can now:

- Map each user to a clear set of permissions through their assigned role.
- Protect any endpoint or service with a one-line permission check.
- Adjust permissions for all users with a given role from a single definition.
- Easily introduce new roles and permissions as our project grows.

Two-Factor Authentication

Although the password security is strong, but passwords alone can be compromised by phishing, leaks, or brute force. If we do have a second proof, like typically a code from the user's phone or a Two-Factor Authentication (2FA), it can drastically reduce the risk of unauthorized account access. Also, the Time-based One-Time Passwords (TOTP) work seamlessly with mobile apps like Google Authenticator, Microsoft Authenticator, or Authy, making 2FA familiar, convenient, and powerful.

Generating and Storing Shared Secret

Each user enabling 2FA needs a unique, secret key shared between our server and their authenticator app. We use the **pyotp** library to generate and validate TOTP codes. First, update our user model to include a **totp_secret** and a boolean for **is_2fa_enabled**:

```
# app/models.py
from sqlalchemy import Column, String, Boolean
class UserModel(Base):
    # ... existing fields ...
    totp_secret = Column(String, nullable=True)
    is_2fa_enabled = Column(Boolean, default=False)
    failed_2fa_attempts = Column(Integer, default=0)
    lockout_until = Column(DateTime, nullable=True)
```

Now, we will build a route to start the 2FA enrollment. When a user opts in, the backend generates a secret, stores it, and returns a QR code to scan.

Provisioning with QR Codes

After generating a TOTP secret, we'll encode it as a QR code so users can scan it into their app. Given below is how the enrollment endpoint works using **pyotp** and **qrcode** libraries:

```
# app/routes/auth.py
import pyotp
import qrcode
import io
import base64
```

```
from fastapi import APIRouter, Depends
from sqlalchemy.orm import Session
from app.models import UserModel
from app.db import get_db
from datetime import datetime
router = APIRouter()
@router.post("/2fa/enroll")
def enroll_2fa(current_user: UserModel =
Depends(get_current_user), db: Session = Depends(get_db)):
    if current_user.is_2fa_enabled:
        return {"msg": "2FA is already enabled"}
    # Generate a new secret
    secret = pyotp.random_base32()
    current_user.totp_secret = secret
    db.commit()
    # Create TOTP provisioning URI
    issuer = "MyApp"
    email = current_user.email
    totp_uri =
pyotp.totp.TOTP(secret).provisioning_uri(name=email,
issuer_name=issuer)
    # Generate QR code as a base64 image
    img = qrcode.make(totp_uri)
    buf = io.BytesIO()
    img.save(buf, format="PNG")
    qr_base64 = base64.b64encode(buf.getvalue()).decode()
    return {
        "qr_code": qr_base64,
        "manual_entry_key": secret,
        "msg": "Scan the QR with our authenticator app."
```

```
}
```

Here, the user receives a base64-encoded PNG for the QR code, which they scan using their chosen authenticator app. The secret is also returned in case manual entry is needed.

Confirming 2FA Enrollment

After scanning, the user enters a TOTP code from their app to confirm setup. We validate the code and enable 2FA as shown below:

```
from pydantic import BaseModel
class TwoFACode(BaseModel):
    code: str
@router.post("/2fa/confirm")
def confirm_2fa(data: TwoFACode, current_user: UserModel =
Depends(get_current_user), db: Session = Depends(get_db)):
    if not current_user.totp_secret:
        return {"msg": "2FA not enrolled"}
    totp = pyotp.TOTP(current_user.totp_secret)
    if totp.verify(data.code):
        current_user.is_2fa_enabled = True
        db.commit()
        return {"msg": "2FA enabled successfully"}
    else:
        return {"msg": "Invalid code, try again"}
```

Only after entering a valid TOTP will the account be marked as 2FA-enabled.

Enforcing 2FA

With 2FA enabled, we need to update the login process. After verifying the password, if the user has 2FA enabled, we require a TOTP code. If the code is missing or invalid, login fails.

For this, we will modify the login route to handle the second factor:

```
from app.security import verify_password
from datetime import timedelta
```

```
@router.post("/login-2fa")
def login_2fa(data: LoginRequest, code: str = "", db: Session = Depends(get_db)):
    user = db.query(UserModel).filter(UserModel.email == data.email).first()
    if not user or not user.is_active:
        raise HTTPException(status_code=401, detail="Invalid credentials or inactive account")
    if user.lockout_until and user.lockout_until > datetime.utcnow():
        raise HTTPException(status_code=403, detail="Account temporarily locked. Try later.")
    if not verify_password(data.password, user.hashed_password):
        raise HTTPException(status_code=401, detail="Invalid credentials")
    # If user has 2FA enabled, require TOTP code
    if user.is_2fa_enabled:
        totp = pyotp.TOTP(user.totp_secret)
        if not code or not totp.verify(code):
            user.failed_2fa_attempts += 1
            if user.failed_2fa_attempts >= 5:
                user.lockout_until = datetime.utcnow() + timedelta(minutes=10)
                user.failed_2fa_attempts = 0
                db.commit()
                raise HTTPException(status_code=403, detail="Too many failed attempts. Locked for 10 minutes.")
            db.commit()
            raise HTTPException(status_code=401, detail="Invalid 2FA code.")
        user.failed_2fa_attempts = 0
```

```
        user.lockout_until = None
        db.commit()
    token = create_jwt_token(user.id, user.email)
    return {"access_token": token, "token_type": "bearer"}
```

You'll see that the route checks if the user is under a lockout, verifies the password, and if 2FA is enabled, validates the code. If you keep trying and it doesn't work, the account is locked for a set period (10 minutes in this example).

With all pieces together, here's what our 2FA-secured login looks like:

1. The user enables 2FA and scans a QR code with their authenticator app.
2. The backend confirms setup by verifying the first TOTP code.
3. On future logins, after verifying their password, users with 2FA enabled must provide the current 6-digit code from their authenticator.
4. The backend checks for lockouts and validates the code. After too many failed attempts, the account is locked, protecting against attacks.
5. A successful login issues a JWT as before, allowing access to protected APIs.

If you'd like to see sample QR code image rendering in the frontend, integration with SMS/email fallback, or real-world alerting on lockouts, those can be layered in.

Summary

Throughout this chapter, we established a secure, professional authentication system for our application. We started by building a robust user registration flow, which issued time-limited email confirmation tokens and handled asynchronous email delivery, ensuring only verified users gained access. Passwords were securely stored using bcrypt hashing, and our login logic enforced credential verification before issuing JWTs for session management. We then implemented password reset capabilities, generating secure, time-bound tokens to facilitate safe credential changes.

With role-based access control, we defined clear permission sets, assigned them to user roles, and enforced access rules at the route level using decorators and dependencies, keeping our logic clean and maintainable. The integration of two-factor authentication brought an extra layer of security, using TOTP secrets, QR code provisioning, and rigorous enforcement of second-factor checks during login. We introduced lockout mechanisms to defend against repeated failed attempts, protecting user accounts from brute-force attacks. Each feature built seamlessly on the previous ones, demonstrating how careful, layered security enables safe, flexible user management for any modern application.

CHAPTER 3: USER EXPERIENCE ENHANCEMENTS

Overview

This chapter's going to teach you how to design and deliver a sophisticated, responsive user experience by adding advanced frontend and backend enhancements to our Python web applications. To get started, you'll build an easy-to-use drag-and-drop file upload interface, where you'll learn to combine real-time feedback and server-side storage, including cloud integration. Next, you'll learn how to use Pydantic to define form schemas and dynamically render forms based on JSON. This'll let you adapt to new requirements and run conditional logic in real time. The chapter will also walk you through dealing with errors with custom Jinja2 templates, so you can provide clear, context-rich messages that are tailored to each situation.

In the next section, you'll learn how to show toast notifications for instant feedback right in the app. This will make it easier for our users to communicate status and error information. To add to our toolkit, you'll learn to set up a professional theme toggle using CSS variables and cookies. This makes sure that user preferences stay the same across sessions and show up right away on the interface.

Drag-and-Drop File Uploads

These days, web apps often ask users to submit files like profile images, documents, or other content. It can feel outdated to rely on classic upload buttons. A well-designed drag-and-drop interface is a better option because it's smoother and more intuitive. We can create a simple, seamless, real-time file upload flow that feels natural on both desktop and mobile by combining a basic JavaScript widget on the front end with strong FastAPI endpoints on the back end. We'll start with a basic, dependency-free JavaScript approach, then move on to the FastAPI upload logic, and finish by connecting the backend to both local storage and cloud destinations like AWS S3.

Designing Frontend Drag-and-Drop

So here, the goal is a visually clear drop area, with live highlighting when a file is dragged over, and instant feedback as the upload progresses. We will keep the interface basic but functional, so the technique is easy to adapt to any styling or framework later.

We start by creating an **`index.html`** file, and inside the **`<body>`**, we then add a **`div`** to serve as the drop area and an element to display upload progress and the resulting file URL:

```
<!DOCTYPE html>
<html lang="en">
<head>
    <meta charset="UTF-8">
```

```
    <title>Drag-and-Drop File Upload</title>
    <style>
        #drop-area {
            border: 2px dashed #888;
            border-radius: 12px;
            width: 400px;
            height: 160px;
            margin: 60px auto;
            display: flex;
            align-items: center;
            justify-content: center;
            color: #666;
            font-size: 18px;
            background: #fafafa;
            transition: background 0.2s;
        }
        #drop-area.active {
            background: #e6f7ff;
            border-color: #1890ff;
            color: #1890ff;
        }
        #progress-container {
            width: 400px;
            margin: 18px auto;
            font-family: monospace;
        }
        #file-url {
            color: #106b21;
            font-size: 16px;
```

```
            word-break: break-all;
        }
    </style>
</head>
<body>
    <div id="drop-area">Drag &amp; drop our file here</div>
    <div id="progress-container"></div>
    <div id="file-url"></div>
    <script src="upload.js"></script>
</body>
</html>
```

This will ensure a clean separation between the drop area, the upload progress, and the returned URL. Styling can be extended later, but the essentials are in place.

Drag-and-Drop and File Upload Logic in JS

With the UI set, we focus on the **upload.js** file, which handles drag-and-drop, manages the AJAX upload, and streams progress updates. The script listens for drag and drop events, highlights the drop area, and sends the file using the Fetch API.

```
// upload.js
const dropArea = document.getElementById('drop-area');
const progressContainer = document.getElementById('progress-container');
const fileUrl = document.getElementById('file-url');
// Highlight drop area on drag events
['dragenter', 'dragover'].forEach(eventName => {
    dropArea.addEventListener(eventName, e => {
        e.preventDefault();
        e.stopPropagation();
        dropArea.classList.add('active');
    });
```

```
});
['dragleave', 'drop'].forEach(eventName => {
    dropArea.addEventListener(eventName, e => {
        e.preventDefault();
        e.stopPropagation();
        dropArea.classList.remove('active');
    });
});
// Handle file drop
dropArea.addEventListener('drop', e => {
    const files = e.dataTransfer.files;
    if (files.length > 0) {
        uploadFile(files[0]);
    }
});
function uploadFile(file) {
    progressContainer.textContent = '';
    fileUrl.textContent = '';
    const xhr = new XMLHttpRequest();
    xhr.open('POST', '/upload', true);
    xhr.upload.onprogress = (e) => {
        if (e.lengthComputable) {
            const percent = Math.round((e.loaded / e.total) *
100);
            progressContainer.textContent = `Uploading:
${percent}% (${e.loaded} / ${e.total} bytes)`;
        }
    };
    xhr.onload = () => {
        if (xhr.status === 200) {
```

```
            progressContainer.textContent = 'Upload
complete!';
            const resp = JSON.parse(xhr.responseText);
            fileUrl.innerHTML = `File URL: <a
href="${resp.url}" target="_blank">${resp.url}</a>`;
        } else {
            progressContainer.textContent = 'Upload failed: '
+ xhr.responseText;
        }
    };
    xhr.onerror = () => {
        progressContainer.textContent = 'An error occurred
during upload.';
    };
    const formData = new FormData();
    formData.append('file', file);
    xhr.send(formData);
}
```

The above script will give users real-time feedback, displaying progress and the final accessible file URL. The **/upload** endpoint will be handled by FastAPI.

Creating FastAPI File Upload Endpoint

On the backend, we create a new upload route that handles incoming files, stores them, and returns a public URL. We start with local file storage, keeping the implementation simple and portable.

In **routes/uploads.py**:

```
from fastapi import APIRouter, File, UploadFile, HTTPException
from fastapi.responses import JSONResponse
from pathlib import Path
import shutil
import uuid
```

```
router = APIRouter()
UPLOAD_DIR = Path("uploads")
UPLOAD_DIR.mkdir(parents=True, exist_ok=True)
@router.post("/upload")
async def upload_file(file: UploadFile = File(...)):
    # Ensure filename is unique
    file_id = str(uuid.uuid4())
    file_ext = Path(file.filename).suffix
    save_path = UPLOAD_DIR / f"{file_id}{file_ext}"
    try:
        with save_path.open("wb") as buffer:
            shutil.copyfileobj(file.file, buffer)
    except Exception:
        raise HTTPException(status_code=500, detail="Failed to
save file")
    # Compose URL (for local, this may be /files/<id>)
    url = f"/files/{file_id}{file_ext}"
    return JSONResponse({"url": url})
```

This code saves each uploaded file with a unique UUID and returns a URL path where the file can be retrieved.

Serving Uploaded Files Locally

For development or local deployments, serving uploaded files is simple with FastAPI's static files support. In our **`main.py`** or app factory, mount the upload directory:

```
from fastapi import FastAPI
from fastapi.staticfiles import StaticFiles
from routes.uploads import router as uploads_router
app = FastAPI()
app.include_router(uploads_router)
```

```
app.mount("/files", StaticFiles(directory="uploads"),
name="files")
```

Now, the URLs returned by the upload endpoint are accessible to users and applications.

The JavaScript we implemented earlier already displays real-time upload progress by listening to the XMLHttpRequest's **onprogress** event. On the backend, the FastAPI's async file handling ensures that uploads are processed efficiently, but note that upload progress streaming is managed client-side—the browser monitors how much data has been sent. For extremely large files or production-grade monitoring, you may consider a websocket-based status API or NGINX's upload modules, but for most applications, this native browser feedback is sufficient.

Storing Files on AWS S3

When scaling beyond local storage, cloud storage like AWS S3 offers reliability, security, and global accessibility. To support S3 uploads, we add the **boto3** library, and for this, we start by setting up our AWS credentials and S3 bucket. Then, we extend the upload logic in **routes/uploads.py** to optionally upload files to S3 as shown below:

```
import os
import boto3
USE_S3 = os.environ.get("USE_S3", "false").lower() == "true"
S3_BUCKET = os.environ.get("S3_BUCKET", "")
S3_CLIENT = boto3.client("s3") if USE_S3 else None
@router.post("/upload")
async def upload_file(file: UploadFile = File(...)):
    file_id = str(uuid.uuid4())
    file_ext = Path(file.filename).suffix
    filename = f"{file_id}{file_ext}"
    if USE_S3 and S3_CLIENT:
        try:
            S3_CLIENT.upload_fileobj(file.file, S3_BUCKET,
filename)
            url =
f"https://{S3_BUCKET}.s3.amazonaws.com/{filename}"
            return JSONResponse({"url": url})
```

```
        except Exception as e:
            raise HTTPException(status_code=500,
detail=f"Failed to upload to S3: {str(e)}")
    else:
        save_path = UPLOAD_DIR / filename
        try:
            with save_path.open("wb") as buffer:
                shutil.copyfileobj(file.file, buffer)
        except Exception:
            raise HTTPException(status_code=500,
detail="Failed to save file")
        url = f"/files/{filename}"
        return JSONResponse({"url": url})
```

after doing this, the switching between local storage and S3 is seamless. We simply just toggle the **USE_S3** environment variable.

With both client and server complete, users can now drag and drop files directly into the browser, see live progress, and receive a working download link on success. On the backend, FastAPI handles uploads, and our logic can store files either locally or on S3, ready for scale.

A user lands on our page, drags a file over the drop area, and sees the highlight appear. As soon as the file is dropped, the upload begins, and a progress bar or percentage updates in real time. When the upload finishes, the resulting URL appears, clickable and ready to use. This workflow minimizes user friction and feels effortless. From the backend perspective, uploads arrive at the FastAPI endpoint, are securely stored, and are made available by direct URL. Switching from local to cloud storage is a matter of configuration—no code changes needed for the frontend.

Dynamic Form Rendering

Most web apps need to collect info from users, like registration details, feedback, product details, or profile settings. Usually, each form is hand-coded in HTML, but this gets tricky when requirements change or forms get more complex. When you represent form definitions as structured data, such as JSON schemas, our app can generate, update, and render forms dynamically without duplicating logic. Since Pydantic is already being used for backend validation, it makes sense to use its models to both validate data and power flexible form rendering. This makes sure that the frontend and backend always "speak the same language."

Defining Form Schema

We'll start by declaring a Pydantic model for the form we want to render. Just picture a basic "Profile" form with different fields and some fields that only show up under certain conditions:

```
# app/schemas.py
from pydantic import BaseModel, EmailStr, Field
from typing import Optional
class ProfileFormSchema(BaseModel):
    name: str = Field(..., title="Full Name", max_length=60)
    email: EmailStr = Field(..., title="Email Address")
    age: Optional[int] = Field(None, title="Age", ge=0,
le=130)
    wants_newsletter: bool = Field(False, title="Subscribe to
Newsletter?")
    newsletter_frequency: Optional[str] = Field(
        None,
        title="Newsletter Frequency",
        description="Visible only if 'wants_newsletter' is
True",
        regex="^(daily|weekly|monthly)$"
    )
```

This schema describes field types, constraints, and titles. The **newsletter_frequency** should only appear if **wants_newsletter** is checked.

Exposing Form Schema as JSON

To allow the frontend to render forms dynamically, we then create a FastAPI endpoint that returns the schema's structure as JSON:

```
# app/routes/forms.py
from fastapi import APIRouter
from app.schemas import ProfileFormSchema
router = APIRouter()
```

```
@router.get("/profile-form-schema")
def get_profile_form_schema():
    return ProfileFormSchema.schema()
```

This endpoint will produce a standard JSON Schema document that fully describes all fields, types, and metadata.

Generating Dynamic HTML Forms

At the front, you can grab the schema with JavaScript. Then you can parse it and generate the right HTML inputs. Below is a quick sample using vanilla JS:

```
<!-- index.html -->
<div id="dynamic-form"></div>
<script>
async function renderForm() {
    const resp = await fetch('/profile-form-schema');
    const schema = await resp.json();
    const container = document.getElementById('dynamic-form');
    container.innerHTML = '';
    for (const [name, props] of
Object.entries(schema.properties)) {
        let input = null;
        if (props.type === 'string' && props.format ===
'email') {
            input = `<input type="email" id="${name}"
name="${name}" placeholder="${props.title || name}">`;
        } else if (props.type === 'string') {
            input = `<input type="text" id="${name}"
name="${name}" placeholder="${props.title || name}">`;
        } else if (props.type === 'integer') {
            input = `<input type="number" id="${name}"
name="${name}" placeholder="${props.title || name}"
min="${props.minimum || ''}" max="${props.maximum || ''}">`;
        } else if (props.type === 'boolean') {
```

```
            input = `<input type="checkbox" id="${name}"
name="${name}"> <label for="${name}">${props.title ||
name}</label>`;
        }
        if (input) {
            container.innerHTML += `<div class="form-field"
id="field-${name}">${input}</div>`;
        }
    }
}
renderForm();
</script>
```

This simple logic renders text, email, number, and checkbox fields based on the schema provided by FastAPI. The **`placeholder`** and labels use the field's title for clarity.

Applying Conditional Visibility Rules

Now, we will add logic so the **`newsletter_frequency`** field only appears if the "Subscribe to Newsletter?" checkbox is checked. This can be achieved by listening to input changes and toggling field visibility:

```
// ...after rendering the fields...
document.getElementById('wants_newsletter').addEventListener('
change', function() {
    const freqField = document.getElementById('field-
newsletter_frequency');
    if (this.checked) {
        freqField.style.display = 'block';
    } else {
        freqField.style.display = 'none';
    }
});
// Hide newsletter_frequency by default
```

```
document.getElementById('field-
newsletter_frequency').style.display = 'none';
```

This ensures conditional rules are respected dynamically—no page reload required. The form instantly adapts as the user interacts.

Submitting and Validating Form

When the user submits the form, gather all field values, including conditionally visible ones, and send them to a FastAPI endpoint. On the backend, the same Pydantic schema validates the data, catching errors and returning feedback.

```
// Example submit handler
async function handleSubmit() {
    const formData = {};
    formData.name = document.getElementById('name').value;
    formData.email = document.getElementById('email').value;
    formData.age =
parseInt(document.getElementById('age').value) || null;
    formData.wants_newsletter =
document.getElementById('wants_newsletter').checked;
    if (formData.wants_newsletter) {
        formData.newsletter_frequency =
document.getElementById('newsletter_frequency').value;
    }
    const resp = await fetch('/submit-profile', {
        method: 'POST',
        headers: {'Content-Type': 'application/json'},
        body: JSON.stringify(formData)
    });
    const result = await resp.json();
    alert(JSON.stringify(result));
}
```

The backend endpoint uses the exact same schema:

```
# app/routes/forms.py
from fastapi import APIRouter
from app.schemas import ProfileFormSchema
router = APIRouter()
@router.post("/submit-profile")
def submit_profile(data: ProfileFormSchema):
    # FastAPI + Pydantic automatically validate and parse
input
    return {"msg": "Profile submitted successfully!", "data":
data.dict()}
```

The best part about this way of building is how flexible it is. And if you need to add a new field, you can do that too. Just tweak the Pydantic schema, and the frontend will instantly reflect the new requirement. Complex forms with nested sections, enums, or additional conditions are just a matter of extending the schema and frontend logic. As soon as the page loads, the schema is fetched, fields are rendered, and the form adapts instantly as users interact. You can add or remove fields in our Pydantic model and watch the frontend adjust. There is no need to mess around with manual HTML rewrites. Every form submission is validated server-side, which guarantees data integrity.

Custom Error Pages & Alerts

Understanding HTTP Error Codes and Their Meanings

Before customizing the user experience around errors, it's valuable to understand what each HTTP error code represents. These codes are standards that browsers, APIs, and users rely on to interpret what went wrong:

- ***400 Bad Request***: The server could not understand the request due to malformed syntax or invalid data.
- ***401 Unauthorized***: The request requires user authentication. Credentials are missing or invalid.
- ***403 Forbidden***: The server understood the request, but refuses to authorize it (insufficient permissions).
- ***404 Not Found***: The requested resource could not be found on the server.
- ***409 Conflict***: The request could not be processed due to a conflict with the current state (e.g., duplicate data).
- ***422 Unprocessable Entity***: The server understands the request but can't process the

contained instructions, often due to validation errors.

- ***500 Internal Server Error***: An unexpected condition was encountered; typically indicates a bug or unhandled edge case.
- ***503 Service Unavailable***: The server is currently unable to handle the request, often due to maintenance or overload.

Creating Custom Jinja2 Error Templates

The FastAPI supports Jinja2 templating for HTML responses. To do this, we first create a directory named **`templates/`**, and inside it, we then add a base template and individual error templates such as ***templates/base.html***:

```
<!DOCTYPE html>
<html lang="en">
<head>
    <meta charset="UTF-8">
    <title>{{ title or "App" }}</title>
    <style>
        body { font-family: sans-serif; margin: 40px; color:
#2b2b2b; }
        .error-container { max-width: 460px; margin: 60px
auto; background: #fff4f4; border-radius: 10px; box-shadow: 0
2px 8px #ececec; padding: 32px; }
        .error-code { font-size: 3em; color: #d35400; }
        .error-message { margin: 12px 0 0 0; font-size: 1.3em;
}
        .error-detail { color: #777; margin-top: 14px; }
        a { color: #1890ff; text-decoration: none; }
    </style>
</head>
<body>
    <div class="error-container">
        {% block content %}{% endblock %}
    </div>
```

```
</body>
</html>
```

And then we create ***templates/error.html***:

```
{% extends "base.html" %}
{% block content %}
    <div class="error-code">{{ code }}</div>
    <div class="error-message">{{ message }}</div>
    {% if detail %}
        <div class="error-detail">{{ detail }}</div>
    {% endif %}
    <div style="margin-top:16px;">
        <a href="/">Return Home</a>
    </div>
{% endblock %}
```

This templates are reusable for any error, injecting the code, a main message, and optional details.

Rendering Custom Error Pages

So, first you'll want to integrate Jinja2 into our FastAPI app, and then use exception handlers to render the correct template. In our **main.py**:

```
from fastapi import FastAPI, Request, status
from fastapi.responses import HTMLResponse
from fastapi.templating import Jinja2Templates
from fastapi.exception_handlers import RequestValidationError
from starlette.exceptions import HTTPException as
StarletteHTTPException
app = FastAPI()
templates = Jinja2Templates(directory="templates")
@app.exception_handler(StarletteHTTPException)
```

```
async def http_exception_handler(request: Request, exc:
StarletteHTTPException):
    context = {
        "request": request,
        "code": exc.status_code,
        "message": {
            404: "Page Not Found",
            403: "Permission Denied",
            401: "Unauthorized",
            500: "Server Error"
        }.get(exc.status_code, "An error occurred"),
        "detail": exc.detail if hasattr(exc, "detail") else ""
    }
    return templates.TemplateResponse("error.html", context,
status_code=exc.status_code)
@app.exception_handler(RequestValidationError)
async def validation_exception_handler(request: Request, exc:
RequestValidationError):
    context = {
        "request": request,
        "code": 422,
        "message": "Invalid Data Submitted",
        "detail": str(exc)
    }
    return templates.TemplateResponse("error.html", context,
status_code=422)
```

Now, whenever a matching error occurs (e.g., a 404), FastAPI automatically renders our custom template with the right code and message.

Context-Aware Error Messages

Sometimes, error details should be personalized, maybe a "not found" page includes the missing resource's name, or a validation error lists which fields failed. You can pass extra context into our error templates directly from the exception handler or by raising custom exceptions:

```
from fastapi import HTTPException
@app.get("/user/{user_id}")
def get_user(user_id: int):
    # Imagine this fetches from a database
    user = None
    if not user:
        raise HTTPException(
            status_code=404,
            detail=f"User with ID {user_id} not found"
        )
```

This **`detail`** will appear in our Jinja2 error template's **`{{ detail }}`** block, making the error more useful and actionable. For more complex context, such as showing suggestions or links, you can extend the template or context dictionary as needed.

In-App Toast Notifications

In modern web apps, instant feedback is often best delivered as toast notifications, which are brief, animated messages that appear above the content. These are perfect for validation errors, success alerts, or warnings that don't warrant a full page.

To do this, we add a notification container to our HTML, then show toasts dynamically:

```
<!-- In our main HTML template, e.g., base.html -->
<div id="toast"
style="display:none;position:fixed;top:18px;right:24px;z-
index:1000;min-width:240px;padding:14px
28px;background:#222;color:#fff;border-radius:6px;box-shadow:0
2px 12px #0003;font-size:1.08em;opacity:0.95;"></div>
```

Now, add a JS function for displaying alerts:

```
// toast.js
function showToast(message, timeout=3200) {
    const toast = document.getElementById('toast');
```

```
    toast.textContent = message;
    toast.style.display = "block";
    setTimeout(() => { toast.style.display = "none"; },
timeout);
}
// Example usage after a fetch or validation error
fetch('/some-endpoint')
  .then(resp => {
    if (!resp.ok) throw new Error("Something went wrong!");
    return resp.json();
  })
  .then(data => {
    showToast("Upload complete!");
  })
  .catch(err => {
    showToast("Failed: " + err.message);
  });
```

With these enhancements, our app becomes resilient, user-friendly, and visually polished. If you wish to extend this further, you can add logging, user feedback tools, or even support for localized error pages using the same techniques.

Theme Toggle

These days, a lot of web apps have a light/dark theme option to make it easier for users to customize their experience. The best way to do this is CSS custom properties ("variables"). They let you switch color schemes instantly, and there is no need to reload or deal with flickering. If you save the user's choice in a cookie and then read it back when the page loads, you make sure their choice sticks, even if they switch sessions or refresh the page. Here's how you put all these pieces together.

Building CSS with Custom Properties

To begin with this, we start with a base stylesheet that defines both light and dark themes using CSS variables at the **`:root`** level. Then, we change the variables under a **`[data-`**

theme="dark"] attribute.

```
<!-- index.html (snippet) -->
<head>
    <style>
        :root {
            --bg: #fafbff;
            --fg: #222;
            --link: #0033ff;
            --panel: #fff;
        }
        [data-theme="dark"] {
            --bg: #23272e;
            --fg: #ededed;
            --link: #66b7ff;
            --panel: #333942;
        }
        body {
            background: var(--bg);
            color: var(--fg);
            transition: background 0.22s, color 0.18s;
            min-height: 100vh;
        }
        .themed-panel {
            background: var(--panel);
            border-radius: 8px;
            padding: 32px;
            margin: 40px auto;
            box-shadow: 0 2px 12px #0001;
            max-width: 520px;
```

```
        }
        a { color: var(--link); }
        .theme-toggle-btn {
            float: right;
            padding: 6px 20px;
            border: none;
            background: var(--panel);
            color: var(--fg);
            border-radius: 6px;
            cursor: pointer;
            font-size: 1em;
            box-shadow: 0 1px 4px #0001;
            margin: 14px;
        }
    </style>
</head>
```

The variables control all the key colors, so toggling themes becomes a matter of switching the **data-theme** attribute on the **<html>** or **<body>** element.

Adding Theme Toggle Button

Just add a simple button at the top of our HTML to switch up the theme.

```
<body>
    <button class="theme-toggle-btn" id="theme-toggle">
Toggle Theme</button>
    <div class="themed-panel">
        <h2>Welcome!</h2>
        <p>This panel follows our selected theme.</p>
    </div>
    <script src="theme.js"></script>
```

```
</body>
```

Implementing Theme Switching

The JavaScript logic will:

- Detect the current theme (by checking the attribute or cookie)
- Switch themes on button click
- Save the preference to a cookie (so it persists)
- On page load, restore the theme from the cookie if present

Following is a simple implementation in **theme.js**:

```
// theme.js
function setTheme(theme) {
    document.documentElement.setAttribute('data-theme',
theme);
}
function getThemeFromCookie() {
    const match = document.cookie.match(/theme=(light|dark)/);
    return match ? match[1] : null;
}
function saveThemeToCookie(theme) {
    // Cookie persists for 1 year, path=/ for all routes
    document.cookie = `theme=${theme}; path=/; max-
age=31536000`;
}
// Toggle between 'light' and 'dark'
function toggleTheme() {
    let current = document.documentElement.getAttribute('data-
theme') || 'light';
    let next = current === 'dark' ? 'light' : 'dark';
    setTheme(next);
    saveThemeToCookie(next);
}
```

```
// On page load, restore theme
window.onload = function() {
    const cookieTheme = getThemeFromCookie();
    setTheme(cookieTheme || 'light');
    document.getElementById('theme-toggle').onclick =
toggleTheme;
};
```

The above logic checks the cookie first, so if a user previously set "dark" mode, the site respects it on every new session.

Managing User Preferences Server-Side

For more advanced setups, like when user authentication is involved, you might want the backend to read or set the theme preference in cookies. The FastAPI makes this easy. Let us consider that you want every page render to include the theme, using server-side templates.

The given below is an example for Jinja2:

```
# main.py or our route file
from fastapi import FastAPI, Request, Response
from fastapi.templating import Jinja2Templates
app = FastAPI()
templates = Jinja2Templates(directory="templates")
@app.get("/")
def home(request: Request):
    theme = request.cookies.get("theme", "light")
    return templates.TemplateResponse("index.html",
{"request": request, "theme": theme})
```

In our Jinja2 template, use the variable to set the attribute:

```
<html lang="en" data-theme="{{ theme }}">
<!-- ... -->
</html>
```

Synchronizing Theme

With cookies, a user's preference is remembered across sessions. If you want to sync theme toggling across multiple browser tabs (for an even smoother experience), you can use **`localStorage`** and a "storage" event listener as shown below:

```
function setTheme(theme) {
    document.documentElement.setAttribute('data-theme',
theme);
    localStorage.setItem('theme', theme);
    saveThemeToCookie(theme);
}
window.addEventListener('storage', (event) => {
    if (event.key === 'theme') {
        setTheme(event.newValue);
    }
});
window.onload = function() {
    const localTheme = localStorage.getItem('theme');
    const cookieTheme = getThemeFromCookie();
    setTheme(localTheme || cookieTheme || 'light');
    document.getElementById('theme-toggle').onclick =
toggleTheme;
};
```

With this, changing the theme in one tab updates it everywhere. This makes our theme experience feel modern and consistent.

Summary

To sum it all up, we developed some features that made it so that our users have a better experience overall on the app. First, we created a drag-and-drop file upload system that made it easy for users to transfer files and gave them real-time progress feedback. They could also access their uploaded content right away through generated URLs, whether it was stored locally or on AWS S3. We then used Pydantic schemas exposed as JSON to implement dynamic form rendering, building a process where HTML forms were generated on the fly and could easily adapt to changing requirements or conditional visibility rules. Then, we looked at how to deal with errors, using custom Jinja2 templates for different HTTP status codes and adding context-aware details. This makes sure that users always see clear, branded, and actionable error messages. We've also added in-app toast notifications for real-time feedback that isn't intrusive. We wrapped up the chapter by adding a theme toggle feature that used CSS custom properties, handled user preferences with cookies and local storage, and synced theme choices across sessions and tabs. All of these improvements made the interface feel modern, trustworthy, and easy to use.

Chapter 4: Notifications & Integrations

Overview

In this chapter, you'll learn how to design and implement advanced notification and integration features that make our Python application interactive and interoperable. We'll start by taking a look at email delivery, going from SMTP configuration to scalable, fault-tolerant background processing with Celery and task monitoring with Flower. Then, you'll use Twilio to set up real-time SMS notification workflows, integrating HTTPX-powered API calls, webhook-based delivery tracking, and strong retry logic to make sure every message makes it through.

The chapter will also walk you through adding OAuth2 social login with Google and GitHub, covering everything from secure token exchanges to syncing user profiles and implementing smooth token refresh. Finally, you'll put together a basic webhook receiver that checks incoming messages using HMAC signatures and safely sends them to Celery for processing. By practicing with these real-world scenarios, you'll pick up the skills to build apps that communicate seamlessly with users and external systems, ensuring reliability, security, and flexibility at every level.

Email Service with Celery

Think about how a solid email service fits into the apps we use today. It's all about the user triggering an action, like signing up, asking for a password reset, or getting an alert. Then the app has to send an email to the user, but if it relies on a direct, synchronous send, the API has to wait for the email to be delivered. If there's network latency, slow servers, or temporary errors, it can mess up the user experience and lead to some pretty risky situations in the user interface.

The typical workflow involves several moving parts:

1. The user performs an action that requires an email (for instance, registration).
2. The FastAPI server processes the request and enqueues an email job in a message broker (often Redis or RabbitMQ).
3. A Celery worker running in the background picks up the email job and sends the email via SMTP.
4. If the email fails (due to a network hiccup or mail server issue), Celery can automatically retry the job as per the configured strategy.
5. An admin or developer can monitor these jobs—seeing successes, failures, or retries—using a tool like Flower, which provides a real-time dashboard.

This above architecture keeps the application fast, reliable, and maintainable, separating time-consuming or failure-prone tasks from the main user flow.

Configuring SMTP Settings

Whenever there's an email sent from our app, it goes through an SMTP server. You can use providers like Gmail, SendGrid, AWS SES, and others. You'll need to keep our credentials, host, port, and connection type safe and secure.

To get started, define these in our settings file or as environment variables:

```
# config.py
import os
SMTP_HOST = os.getenv("SMTP_HOST", "smtp.example.com")
SMTP_PORT = int(os.getenv("SMTP_PORT", 587))
SMTP_USERNAME = os.getenv("SMTP_USERNAME", "your_username")
SMTP_PASSWORD = os.getenv("SMTP_PASSWORD", "your_password")
SMTP_USE_TLS = os.getenv("SMTP_USE_TLS", "true").lower() in
("1", "true", "yes")
FROM_EMAIL = os.getenv("FROM_EMAIL", "no-reply@example.com")
```

These settings allow our email logic to remain generic and easily portable to any provider.

Next, we then write a utility to send an email using Python's standard library, **smtplib** to actually send the email as shown below:

```
# app/email_utils.py
import smtplib
from email.mime.text import MIMEText
from email.mime.multipart import MIMEMultipart
from config import SMTP_HOST, SMTP_PORT, SMTP_USERNAME,
SMTP_PASSWORD, SMTP_USE_TLS, FROM_EMAIL
def send_email(to_email, subject, html_body, plain_body=None):
    msg = MIMEMultipart("alternative")
    msg["From"] = FROM_EMAIL
    msg["To"] = to_email
    msg["Subject"] = subject
    part1 = MIMEText(plain_body or html_body, "plain")
    part2 = MIMEText(html_body, "html")
    msg.attach(part1)
    msg.attach(part2)
    with smtplib.SMTP(SMTP_HOST, SMTP_PORT) as server:
```

```
        if SMTP_USE_TLS:
            server.starttls()
        server.login(SMTP_USERNAME, SMTP_PASSWORD)
        server.sendmail(FROM_EMAIL, to_email, msg.as_string())
```

This function builds a MIME email with both plain text and HTML, connects to the SMTP server, and sends the message. For production systems, always keep credentials secure and handle exceptions for resilience.

Celery for Asynchronous Email Dispatch

We know that the Celery allows to process tasks in the background, outside of the web request/response cycle. So here, we will need both Celery and a message broker such as Redis. Incase, you have not installed earlier, follow the below step to quickly get them installed:

```
pip install celery redis
```

We then configure Celery in our project:

```
# app/celery_worker.py
from celery import Celery
CELERY_BROKER_URL = "redis://localhost:6379/0"
CELERY_RESULT_BACKEND = CELERY_BROKER_URL
celery_app = Celery(
    "email_tasks",
    broker=CELERY_BROKER_URL,
    backend=CELERY_RESULT_BACKEND
)
```

Next, we then define a Celery task for sending email:

```
# app/tasks.py
from app.celery_worker import celery_app
from app.email_utils import send_email
@celery_app.task(bind=True, max_retries=3,
default_retry_delay=30)
```

```
def send_email_task(self, to_email, subject, html_body, plain_body=None):
    try:
        send_email(to_email, subject, html_body, plain_body)
    except Exception as exc:
        # Retry the task automatically if email sending fails
        raise self.retry(exc=exc)
```

With this setup, our FastAPI routes can simply enqueue an email send job and return to the user instantly. It will delegate all email-related work to Celery.

Triggering Email Tasks

If something happens (like a user signing up), it's better to enqueue the Celery task instead of sending the email right away as below:

```
# app/routes/notifications.py
from fastapi import APIRouter
from app.tasks import send_email_task
router = APIRouter()
@router.post("/register")
def register_user(email: str):
    # ... registration logic ...
    subject = "Welcome!"
    html_body = "<h3>Thank you for signing up!</h3>"
    send_email_task.delay(email, subject, html_body)
    return {"msg": "Registration complete. Please check our email."}
```

The **`.delay()`** method places the task in the Redis queue, and the Celery worker picks it up as soon as possible.

Monitoring Celery Tasks

The Flower is a web-based tool for monitoring Celery jobs in real time. You can track successful deliveries, failed attempts, retries, and queue status, thus making it invaluable for production support.

To run the Flower, do the following:

```
pip install flower
celery -A app.celery_worker.celery_app flower --port=5555
```

Next, then open *http://localhost:5555* in our browser. After you open it, you can see:

- ***Active Tasks***: Jobs currently being processed
- ***Succeeded/Failed Tasks***: Immediate visibility into the results
- ***Retries***: Email jobs that failed (e.g., SMTP server was temporarily unreachable) and will be retried automatically
- ***Task Details***: Click into any task to see full context and traceback if it failed

This makes it easy to troubleshoot and audit our notification pipeline without sifting through log files.

By following all these steps, we've made a modern email service for our app that's production-grade. It can handle a lot of emails at once, automatically try again if something goes wrong, and we're monitoring it all in real time. And it's all powered by Python, Celery, and Flower.

SMS Notifications via Twilio

Modern applications often require real-time notifications—not just by email, but also through SMS, which is more immediate and more likely to be seen. Twilio is one of the industry standards for sending and tracking SMS worldwide. In a robust design, SMS delivery should never block the main app or API—messages are queued with Celery, sent asynchronously via HTTPX, and monitored for delivery status via Twilio's webhooks. Retries are built-in, ensuring the user experience is reliable and responsive.

Configuring Twilio Credentials and Settings

Now here, to send the SMS, we need to have the Twilio account credentials: **ACCOUNT_SID**, **AUTH_TOKEN**, and a registered **FROM_NUMBER**. We need to store these as environment variables for security as shown below:

```
# config.py
import os
TWILIO_ACCOUNT_SID = os.getenv("TWILIO_ACCOUNT_SID")
TWILIO_AUTH_TOKEN = os.getenv("TWILIO_AUTH_TOKEN")
TWILIO_FROM_NUMBER = os.getenv("TWILIO_FROM_NUMBER")
```

```
TWILIO_API_URL = f"https://api.twilio.com/2010-04-01/Accounts/{TWILIO_ACCOUNT_SID}/Messages.json"
```

Sending SMS with HTTPX

Instead of the official SDK, you use HTTPX for async, lightweight requests. Given below is a reusable utility function to send an SMS using HTTP Basic Auth:

```
# app/sms_utils.py
import httpx
from config import TWILIO_ACCOUNT_SID, TWILIO_AUTH_TOKEN, TWILIO_FROM_NUMBER, TWILIO_API_URL
async def send_sms_via_twilio(to_number: str, body: str, status_callback_url: str = None):
    data = {
        "From": TWILIO_FROM_NUMBER,
        "To": to_number,
        "Body": body,
    }
    if status_callback_url:
        data["StatusCallback"] = status_callback_url
    async with httpx.AsyncClient() as client:
        resp = await client.post(
            TWILIO_API_URL,
            data=data,
            auth=(TWILIO_ACCOUNT_SID, TWILIO_AUTH_TOKEN)
        )
        resp.raise_for_status()
        return resp.json()
```

The **StatusCallback** URL tells Twilio where to POST delivery receipts—vital for tracking if our SMS was delivered, failed, or queued.

Enqueueing SMS Sending

To prevent delays or bottlenecks, the SMS jobs are processed asynchronously by Celery. Following is how you define the task:

```
# app/tasks.py
from app.celery_worker import celery_app
from app.sms_utils import send_sms_via_twilio
import asyncio
@celery_app.task(bind=True, max_retries=4,
default_retry_delay=40)
def send_sms_task(self, to_number, message,
status_callback_url=None):
    try:
        # Run the async function in the event loop (since
Celery tasks are sync)
        loop = asyncio.get_event_loop()
        result = loop.run_until_complete(
            send_sms_via_twilio(to_number, message,
status_callback_url)
        )
        return result
    except Exception as exc:
        raise self.retry(exc=exc)
```

Every SMS notification including the password reset, 2FA code, or alert, now flows through a background task, leaving the main API snappy and resilient.

Handling Twilio Webhook Callbacks

The Twilio can POST real-time status updates about our SMS (queued, sent, delivered, failed) to any HTTPS endpoint you specify. This lets our app track actual delivery, notify users, or trigger alerts if messages bounce.

So here, we now set up a FastAPI route to handle these webhooks:

```
# app/routes/webhooks.py
from fastapi import APIRouter, Request, status
```

```
from fastapi.responses import JSONResponse
router = APIRouter()
@router.post("/webhooks/twilio-sms-status")
async def twilio_sms_status_webhook(request: Request):
    data = await request.form()
    message_sid = data.get("MessageSid")
    message_status = data.get("MessageStatus")
    to_number = data.get("To")
    # Log or update delivery status in the database as needed
    print(f"Twilio SMS: {message_sid} to {to_number} is now
{message_status}")
    # Optionally, update user notification status in DB here
    return JSONResponse({"status": "received"},
status_code=status.HTTP_200_OK)
```

After this, we register this route and provide the URL as **`status_callback_url`** when sending SMS.

Monitoring and Retrying Failed Deliveries

The Celery's retry logic is already built into our task definition. If an SMS send attempt fails, perhaps Twilio returns a 500 error, or the network is temporarily down, the task is retried automatically (up to four times, 40 seconds apart). All retry attempts and results appear in the Celery/Flower dashboard, so operators have real-time visibility and can respond to persistent issues.

Now, I will walk through you the entire complete flow:

1. The app receives an event requiring SMS notification (for example, a login confirmation or alert).
2. FastAPI enqueues the job with Celery—**`send_sms_task.delay(to_number, message, status_callback_url)`**.
3. A Celery worker picks up the task, invokes the async Twilio API call via HTTPX, and receives an immediate response (queued or accepted).
4. If Twilio's API call fails, Celery automatically retries as per our configuration.
5. Twilio sends asynchronous POST requests to our webhook endpoint, updating the delivery status.
6. The app logs, stores, or acts on delivery receipts, keeping users and operators

informed.

This pattern guarantees reliability, transparency, and scalability in our SMS workflows. The flow is highly extensible, and ready for more notification channels, user preferences, or custom alerting logic as our platform grows.

OAuth2 Social Login

To make it easier for users to log in, we're letting them use their trusted third-party accounts, like Google or GitHub. It's a breeze to use, and it cuts down on the hassle of creating new passwords. Plus, it boosts signup rates and uses secure identity providers that we know work well. OAuth2, the protocol used by most major platforms, involves a handshake where users are redirected to the provider, approve our app's request, and are then redirected back with a code that our backend exchanges for access tokens. It lets you verify who the user is, access their profile, and keep the session going without having the user do much.

Registering App with Google/GitHub

Before you can use OAuth2, we need to register the application with both Google and GitHub.

- For ***Google***, use the Google Developer Console, create OAuth credentials, and set the ***Authorized Redirect URL***.
- For ***GitHub***, register at *GitHub Developer Settings*, and set the callback URL (e.g., **`https://yourdomain.com/auth/github/callback`**).

After this, take note of the ***client ID*** and ***client secret*** for each provider, and configure them in environment variables or a secure config as below:

```
# config.py
import os
GOOGLE_CLIENT_ID = os.getenv("GOOGLE_CLIENT_ID")
GOOGLE_CLIENT_SECRET = os.getenv("GOOGLE_CLIENT_SECRET")
GOOGLE_REDIRECT_URI = os.getenv("GOOGLE_REDIRECT_URI",
"http://localhost:8000/auth/google/callback")
GITHUB_CLIENT_ID = os.getenv("GITHUB_CLIENT_ID")
GITHUB_CLIENT_SECRET = os.getenv("GITHUB_CLIENT_SECRET")
GITHUB_REDIRECT_URI = os.getenv("GITHUB_REDIRECT_URI",
"http://localhost:8000/auth/github/callback")
```

Initiating OAuth2 Login Flow

When a user clicks "Sign in with Google" or "Sign in with GitHub," our frontend redirects them to the provider's authorization URL with the required parameters.

Following is an example FastAPI route to start the Google login:

```
# app/routes/oauth2.py
from fastapi import APIRouter
from fastapi.responses import RedirectResponse
from config import GOOGLE_CLIENT_ID, GOOGLE_REDIRECT_URI
router = APIRouter()
@router.get("/auth/google/login")
def login_with_google():
    scope = "openid email profile"
    auth_url = (
        f"https://accounts.google.com/o/oauth2/v2/auth?"
        f"client_id={GOOGLE_CLIENT_ID}"
        f"&redirect_uri={GOOGLE_REDIRECT_URI}"
        f"&response_type=code"
        f"&scope={scope}"
        f"&access_type=offline"
        f"&prompt=consent"
    )
    return RedirectResponse(auth_url)
```

For GitHub, the flow is similar but with a different endpoint and scope string:

```
from config import GITHUB_CLIENT_ID, GITHUB_REDIRECT_URI
@router.get("/auth/github/login")
def login_with_github():
    scope = "read:user user:email"
    auth_url = (
        f"https://github.com/login/oauth/authorize?"
        f"client_id={GITHUB_CLIENT_ID}"
```

```
        f"&redirect_uri={GITHUB_REDIRECT_URI}"
        f"&scope={scope}"
    )
    return RedirectResponse(auth_url)
```

Handling Authorization Callback and Exchanging Code for Tokens

After user consent, Google or GitHub redirects to our callback URL with a **code** parameter. The backend must now exchange this code for access and (optionally) refresh tokens using HTTPX.

Following is an example of Google Token Exchange:

```
import httpx
from config import GOOGLE_CLIENT_ID, GOOGLE_CLIENT_SECRET,
GOOGLE_REDIRECT_URI
@router.get("/auth/google/callback")
async def google_callback(code: str):
    token_url = "https://oauth2.googleapis.com/token"
    data = {
        "client_id": GOOGLE_CLIENT_ID,
        "client_secret": GOOGLE_CLIENT_SECRET,
        "code": code,
        "redirect_uri": GOOGLE_REDIRECT_URI,
        "grant_type": "authorization_code"
    }
    async with httpx.AsyncClient() as client:
        resp = await client.post(token_url, data=data)
        resp.raise_for_status()
        tokens = resp.json()
        access_token = tokens["access_token"]
        refresh_token = tokens.get("refresh_token")
```

```
        id_token = tokens.get("id_token")
```

And, the below one is the GitHub Token Exchange:

```
from config import GITHUB_CLIENT_ID, GITHUB_CLIENT_SECRET, GITHUB_REDIRECT_URI
@router.get("/auth/github/callback")
async def github_callback(code: str):
    token_url = "https://github.com/login/oauth/access_token"
    data = {
        "client_id": GITHUB_CLIENT_ID,
        "client_secret": GITHUB_CLIENT_SECRET,
        "code": code,
        "redirect_uri": GITHUB_REDIRECT_URI
    }
    headers = {"Accept": "application/json"}
    async with httpx.AsyncClient() as client:
        resp = await client.post(token_url, data=data, headers=headers)
        resp.raise_for_status()
        tokens = resp.json()
        access_token = tokens["access_token"]
```

Retrieving and Synchronizing User Profile Information

With the access token, you can now fetch user details. For Google, use the "userinfo" endpoint; for GitHub, use their user API.

```
async with httpx.AsyncClient() as client:
    userinfo_resp = await client.get(
        "https://www.googleapis.com/oauth2/v3/userinfo",
        headers={"Authorization": f"Bearer {access_token}"}
    )
```

```
    userinfo = userinfo_resp.json()
    # Extract fields: sub (user ID), email, name, picture,
etc.
```

And, for the GitHub Profile:

```
async with httpx.AsyncClient() as client:
    userinfo_resp = await client.get(
        "https://api.github.com/user",
        headers={"Authorization": f"Bearer {access_token}"}
    )
    userinfo = userinfo_resp.json()
    # Extract login, id, email, avatar_url, etc.
```

We then synchronize with the user database:

- If the user already exists (matched by provider ID or email), update their profile info.
- If new, create a user record with the fetched info.
- Issue our own session or JWT for our app, linking the social account.

Implementing Token Refresh

The OAuth2 tokens are often short-lived. Google, for example, provides a **refresh_token** (if **access_type=offline** and **prompt=consent** are set) that you can use to obtain a new **access_token** without re-prompting the user. The GitHub access tokens are typically long-lived but can be revoked.

Following is how we refersh the Google Access Token:

```
async def refresh_google_token(refresh_token):
    token_url = "https://oauth2.googleapis.com/token"
    data = {
        "client_id": GOOGLE_CLIENT_ID,
        "client_secret": GOOGLE_CLIENT_SECRET,
        "refresh_token": refresh_token,
        "grant_type": "refresh_token"
    }
```

```
    async with httpx.AsyncClient() as client:
        resp = await client.post(token_url, data=data)
        resp.raise_for_status()
        tokens = resp.json()
        return tokens["access_token"]
```

In the above,

- We store the refresh token securely.
- when the access token expires (e.g., after one hour), call this function to obtain a new one.
- We then use the refreshed token for subsequent API requests.

For our app, we store token expiry and refresh token in the user session or database, thereby refreshing as needed behind the scenes.

The overall experience is as follows:

1. User clicks "Sign in with Google/GitHub."
2. The app redirects to the provider's consent screen.
3. Upon approval, the user is redirected back to our backend's callback.
4. The backend exchanges the code for tokens using HTTPX.
5. The app fetches user profile information and synchronizes it with our user system.
6. User is logged in and issued a session or JWT—no password required.
7. When tokens expire, refresh logic keeps the connection alive.

This flow can be extended to other providers with only minor adjustments, using the same pattern of authorization, token exchange, and profile sync.

Webhook Receiver Handling

The Webhooks are essential for integrating the app with external systems; payment processors, CI/CD pipelines, messaging platforms, or third-party APIs. The webhook provider sends HTTP requests (usually POST) to our endpoint every time an event happens. The app must verify the authenticity, parse the event, and trigger follow-up actions, preferably outside the main request cycle, to avoid timeouts or failures.

For this, we will design an endpoint **`/webhooks/receiver`** that can accept webhooks from multiple services, validate security signatures, and hand off processing work to Celery for reliability and speed.

Creating Webhook Endpoint

To start with, we first add a new router for webhooks in our FastAPI project. The endpoint will accept any JSON payload and headers:

```
# app/routes/webhooks.py
from fastapi import APIRouter, Request, Header, HTTPException,
status
from fastapi.responses import JSONResponse
router = APIRouter()
@router.post("/webhooks/receiver")
async def receive_webhook(
    request: Request,
    x_signature: str = Header(None)  # Example: header name
depends on the provider
):
    payload = await request.body()
    headers = dict(request.headers)
    # Downstream: validate signature, process payload
    # ...
    return JSONResponse({"received": True})
```

This design allows our endpoint to be adapted easily for different webhook standards, and just add or modify header parsing as needed.

Validating HMAC Signatures

Most providers (Stripe, GitHub, Twilio, etc.) include a cryptographic signature in the headers, generated with a secret you set in their dashboard. The job is to re-compute the HMAC over the received body using our secret and compare it to the received signature.

For example, suppose our secret is stored securely:

```
# config.py
import os
WEBHOOK_SECRET = os.getenv("WEBHOOK_SECRET", "supersecret")
```

Now, we then add signature validation using **hmac** and **hashlib**:

```
import hmac
```

```
import hashlib
def validate_signature(payload: bytes, header_signature: str,
secret: str) -> bool:
    # Provider-specific: may use sha1, sha256, or another algo
and header format
    expected_signature = hmac.new(
        secret.encode(), msg=payload, digestmod=hashlib.sha256
    ).hexdigest()
    return hmac.compare_digest(header_signature,
expected_signature)
```

And then finally, we call this function in our endpoint before processing:

```
@router.post("/webhooks/receiver")
async def receive_webhook(
    request: Request,
    x_signature: str = Header(None)
):
    payload = await request.body()
    if not x_signature:
        raise HTTPException(status_code=400, detail="Missing
signature header")
    if not validate_signature(payload, x_signature,
WEBHOOK_SECRET):
        raise HTTPException(status_code=401, detail="Invalid
signature")
    # Proceed to downstream processing
    return JSONResponse({"verified": True})
```

We can adjust the signature algorithm, header name, and construction logic to match the specific provider's docs (some prefix with **sha256=**, etc.).

Enqueuing Celery Tasks for Asynchronous Downstream Processing

After validating the webhook, we then offload any resource-intensive or time-consuming business logic to a Celery task, such as updating a database, notifying users, or syncing with another system. This keeps the webhook handler responsive and robust even under load or during third-party outages.

So here, we first define our Celery task:

```
# app/tasks.py
from app.celery_worker import celery_app
@celery_app.task
def process_webhook_task(event_type, payload):
    # Custom logic depending on event_type, data content, etc.
    print(f"Processing webhook event: {event_type}")
    # For example, update models, trigger follow-up
notifications, etc.
```

In our endpoint, after successful validation, we then parse the payload and enqueue the task:

```
import json
from app.tasks import process_webhook_task
@router.post("/webhooks/receiver")
async def receive_webhook(
    request: Request,
    x_signature: str = Header(None)
):
    payload = await request.body()
    if not x_signature or not validate_signature(payload,
x_signature, WEBHOOK_SECRET):
        raise HTTPException(status_code=401, detail="Invalid
or missing signature")
    event = json.loads(payload)
    event_type = event.get("type", "generic_event")
    process_webhook_task.delay(event_type, event)
    return JSONResponse({"enqueued": True})
```

This pattern works for any webhook payload, regardless of provider. For critical robustness, you may:

- Log every received webhook and its status.
- Add provider-specific logic for signature schemes or event types.
- Use Flower or another Celery dashboard for real-time monitoring and troubleshooting.

With this architecture, the app is ready to integrate safely and efficiently with any external system, scaling smoothly as our traffic and use cases grow. The same techniques apply to GitHub, Stripe, payment processors, and countless other webhook-powered workflows.

Summary

To wrap things up, we've set up a solid base for dealing with notifications and external integrations in our app. We started by looking at how a modern email service works, then set up SMTP and added Celery to handle email dispatch, keep track of retries, and monitor task health using Flower. We moved on to using Twilio for SMS notifications, HTTPX for efficient API calls, and we extended our workflow to process delivery receipts in real time through webhook endpoints. This makes the system responsive and reliable even in the face of temporary failures thanks to automated retries.

Then, we worked on OAuth2-based social login, building out the complete Google and GitHub authentication flows, exchanging codes for tokens, getting and syncing user profile information, and adding secure token refresh logic to make sure user sessions weren't interrupted. At last, we came up with a flexible webhook receiver endpoint that checks HMAC signatures for secure integrations. This lets our app safely accept, verify, and queue incoming webhooks for downstream processing via Celery.

CHAPTER 5: PERFORMANCE & SCALABILITY

Overview

This chapter will teach you how to boost the app's performance and scalability to new heights, making sure it keeps up its top-notch performance as demand and data volume rise. You will start by learning how to use Redis as a caching layer to speed up functions and API routes. You will also learn practical ways to ensure data is accurate and timely.

The chapter will walk you through designing robust rate limiting, letting you track usage for every IP or authenticated user and implement both fixed window and sliding window algorithms. This will ensure that our platform remains fair, available, and protected under heavy load. You will learn how to configure Celery and Redis as a background job engine that can handle everything from intensive report generation to automated cleanups. You will also learn how to chain jobs into seamless workflows. In the final section, Python's async programming model will be explored, where real endpoints will be converted to async, I/O operations will be run concurrently with HTTPX, and the direct impact on user experience will be observed.

Redis-Backed Caching

As an application begins to scale, one of the first performance bottlenecks arises from repeated, redundant computations or costly database queries. We can reduce backend workload, minimize response times, and serve more users efficiently by introducing a dedicated caching layer. This will allow us to do so without incurring unnecessary scaling costs for our infrastructure. In this space, Redis is distinguished by its blazing speed, in-memory data structures, rich feature set, and robust TTL (Time-To-Live) management. Unlike in-process caches, Redis operates as a centralized, persistent service, making it ideal for multi-instance applications and distributed systems.

We can sidestep the pitfalls of local memory caches. These pitfalls include stale data across server nodes or loss of cache after process restarts. We can do this by leveraging Redis. Redis enables us to cache anything, including API responses, database records, and computed function outputs. It also allows us to instantly share those results with all instances of our app.

Connecting FastAPI with Redis

The Redis speaks its own protocol, and with Python's asynchronous capabilities, we want a non-blocking client to keep our web service highly responsive. For this, **aioredis** is an excellent fit—offering async/await support, connection pooling, and native compatibility with FastAPI.

At first, we start by importing **aioredis** and setting up a singleton connection pool in our app. This ensures all requests reuse existing connections efficiently.

```
# app/redis_client.py
import aioredis
```

```
import os
REDIS_URL = os.getenv("REDIS_URL", "redis://localhost:6379/0")
redis = None
async def get_redis():
    global redis
    if redis is None:
        redis = await aioredis.from_url(REDIS_URL,
encoding="utf-8", decode_responses=True)
    return redis
```

This utility prepares us for both small and large deployments—allowing configuration by environment variable and lazy, on-demand connection.

Implementing Function-Level Caching

The function-level caching stores the result of an expensive or frequently called function, keyed by its input arguments, so repeated calls can be served instantly from Redis. This pattern is ideal for pure or mostly pure functions—such as calculations, slow queries, or third-party API calls.

Here, we will create a simple decorator to cache any async function's result in Redis:

```
# app/cache_utils.py
import functools
import json
from app.redis_client import get_redis
def redis_cache(key_template: str, ttl: int = 300):
    """
    Caches the output of an async function in Redis.
    key_template: String, e.g., 'myfunc:{arg1}:{arg2}'
    ttl: Time-to-live in seconds
    """
    def decorator(func):
        @functools.wraps(func)
        async def wrapper(*args, **kwargs):
```

```
            cache_key = key_template.format(*args, **kwargs)
            redis = await get_redis()
            cached = await redis.get(cache_key)
            if cached is not None:
                return json.loads(cached)
            result = await func(*args, **kwargs)
            await redis.set(cache_key, json.dumps(result),
ex=ttl)
            return result
        return wrapper
    return decorator
```

Following is how you might use this decorator to cache the result of a slow function:

```
@redis_cache('user_profile:{user_id}', ttl=600)
async def fetch_user_profile(user_id: int):
    # Simulate database or API call
    await asyncio.sleep(2)
    return {"user_id": user_id, "profile": "Sample user
profile"}
```

On the first call, the function runs as normal; on subsequent calls with the same arguments, Redis instantly provides the cached result, dramatically improving latency.

Adding Route-Level Caching

Sometimes, we want to cache entire HTTP responses—especially for GET endpoints that fetch data infrequently updated, such as public pages or slow reports. By integrating caching at the route level, we can serve repeated client requests with minimal computation.

We will implement a FastAPI dependency that handles caching for a route:

```
from fastapi import Request, Response
from app.redis_client import get_redis
async def cache_response(request: Request, ttl: int = 120):
    redis = await get_redis()
```

```
    cache_key =
f"route_cache:{request.url.path}?{request.url.query}"
    cached = await redis.get(cache_key)
    if cached:
        return Response(content=cached,
media_type="application/json")
    return None  # No cached response
```

Now, in our route, check the cache before running the normal logic, and save the response afterward:

```
from fastapi import APIRouter, Request, Response, status
import json
router = APIRouter()
@router.get("/expensive-resource")
async def get_expensive_resource(request: Request):
    cached_response = await cache_response(request, ttl=180)
    if cached_response:
        return cached_response
    # Simulate slow operation
    await asyncio.sleep(3)
    data = {"expensive": "This result is cached for 3
minutes."}
    # Cache the result in Redis
    redis = await get_redis()
    cache_key =
f"route_cache:{request.url.path}?{request.url.query}"
    await redis.set(cache_key, json.dumps(data), ex=180)
    return data
```

With this setup, the route only recomputes data when the cache has expired or has been explicitly invalidated.

Managing TTL for Cache Entries

We already learnt previously that the TTL is a crucial tool for controlling cache freshness. By specifying an expiration in seconds (**ex**), we ensure that data automatically invalidates after a defined window—no manual cleanup or risk of serving stale responses indefinitely.

In both the function and route-level decorators, you can adjust the **ttl** argument to suit our needs:

- Short TTL (30–120 seconds): for fast-changing data or time-sensitive API results.
- Medium TTL (5–30 minutes): for user dashboards, search results, or periodic reports.
- Long TTL (hours or days): for static content, documentation, or rarely changing reference data.

The Redis handles expiration automatically, evicting expired keys and keeping memory use predictable.

Designing Invalidation Strategies

Sometimes, you need more control, like forcing a cache refresh when underlying data changes, or purging specific entries in response to user actions. Redis makes this easy with key deletion and pattern matching.

Suppose a user updates their profile. After saving to the database, explicitly remove the cache entry for that user:

```
redis = await get_redis()
await redis.delete(f"user_profile:{user_id}")
```

For batch invalidation such as clearing all route-level caches after a bulk update, you can use Redis SCAN or KEYS with a prefix:

```
async def invalidate_all_route_caches():
    redis = await get_redis()
    keys = await redis.keys("route_cache:*")
    if keys:
        await redis.delete(*keys)
```

By combining TTL-based expiration with targeted invalidation, you maintain a fine balance between blazing-fast responses and up-to-date information. For distributed deployments, Redis handles all the app instances seamlessly, so the cache always reflects the current state across our cluster.

Rate Limiting & Throttling

Any solid, flexible app has to have a way to stop its resources from being overloaded or misused, or from getting hit with a sudden surge in traffic. Rate limiting, also known as throttling, is a way to limit the number of requests made by users, clients, or IP addresses within a set time period. This keeps the backend safe from brute-force attacks, spamming, scraping, and basic misconfigurations. It also provides a fair share of resources to all users, keeps things running smoothly, and helps keep response times consistent, even when the application is under load.

To do effective rate limiting, you need to keep track of request counts and time intervals in real time. Storing these counters in Redis gives us both speed and global consistency. Every instance of our application can read and update usage data, ensuring that limits are enforced no matter where the user connects from. There are two main approaches that are used a lot: the ***fixed window*** and ***sliding window*** algorithms, each with trade-offs in accuracy and burst tolerance.

Tracking Requests

To rate limit requests, we must count the number of hits for each key (IP address or user ID) within our chosen time window. So to do this, we first try to create a utility that generates the correct rate-limiting key based on the request. For anonymous clients, we'll use their IP address; for logged-in users, their user ID:

```
# app/rate_limiter.py
from fastapi import Request
def get_rate_limit_key(request: Request, user_id: int = None,
window: str = "minute"):
    if user_id:
        identifier = f"user:{user_id}"
    else:
        identifier = f"ip:{request.client.host}"
    return f"ratelimit:{identifier}:{window}"
```

Fixed Window Rate Limiting Algorithm

The fixed window approach tracks the number of requests in a strict interval (e.g., every minute). When the window resets, so do the counters. It is simple and memory efficient, but may allow short bursts at the boundary of windows.

Following is how to enforce a fixed window using Redis' **INCR** and **EXPIRE**:

```
import time
from fastapi import HTTPException, Request, status
from app.redis_client import get_redis
async def fixed_window_rate_limit(request: Request, user_id: int = None, limit: int = 100, window_seconds: int = 60):
    redis = await get_redis()
    key = get_rate_limit_key(request, user_id, window="minute")
    current_count = await redis.incr(key)
    if current_count == 1:
        await redis.expire(key, window_seconds)
    if current_count > limit:
        ttl = await redis.ttl(key)
        raise HTTPException(
            status_code=status.HTTP_429_TOO_MANY_REQUESTS,
            detail="Too many requests. Please try again later.",
            headers={"Retry-After": str(ttl if ttl > 0 else window_seconds)},
        )
```

In the above,

- On each request, increment the counter for the user or IP.
- If this is the first request in the window, set the expiration to match the window size.
- If the count exceeds the limit, return an HTTP 429 error with a **`Retry-After`** header, telling the client how many seconds remain until the window resets.

Sliding Window Rate Limiting Algorithm

The sliding window algorithm allows for more precise, fair limiting by tracking each individual request's timestamp. The count is checked for the last N seconds, not just a fixed interval. This method helps smooth out bursts and avoids the "boundary" effect of fixed windows.

Here, we can implement this with sorted sets (**`ZADD`**, **`ZREMRANGEBYSCORE`**, **`ZCARD`**):

```
async def sliding_window_rate_limit(request: Request, user_id: int = None, limit: int = 100, window_seconds: int = 60):
    redis = await get_redis()
    key = get_rate_limit_key(request, user_id, window="sliding")
    now = int(time.time())
    window_start = now - window_seconds
    # Add the current timestamp to the sorted set
    await redis.zadd(key, {str(now): now})
    # Remove entries outside the window
    await redis.zremrangebyscore(key, 0, window_start)
    # Count entries in window
    req_count = await redis.zcard(key)
    # Set TTL for automatic cleanup
    await redis.expire(key, window_seconds)
    if req_count > limit:
        # Find when the earliest allowed request will expire
        oldest = await redis.zrange(key, 0, 0, withscores=True)
        if oldest and len(oldest[0]) > 1:
            retry_after = window_seconds - (now - int(float(oldest[0][1])))
        else:
            retry_after = window_seconds
        raise HTTPException(
            status_code=status.HTTP_429_TOO_MANY_REQUESTS,
            detail="Rate limit exceeded. Please try again later.",
            headers={"Retry-After": str(max(1, int(retry_after)))},
        )
```

This technique allows more accurate, "rolling" windows. The clients cannot bypass limits with bursts near the interval boundary.

Rate Limiting to FastAPI Routes

We can integrate our rate limiter as a dependency or a middleware in FastAPI routes. For example, here's how you'd apply it to an endpoint:

```
from fastapi import APIRouter, Request, Depends
router = APIRouter()
@router.get("/public-data")
async def public_data(request: Request):
    await fixed_window_rate_limit(request, limit=20,
window_seconds=60)
    # or: await sliding_window_rate_limit(request, limit=20,
window_seconds=60)
    return {"data": "This endpoint is rate-limited to 20
requests per minute per client."}
```

For user-authenticated endpoints, pass the user ID instead of IP to enforce user-level quotas.

Standardized Retry-After Headers

When a client exceeds their quota, the rate limiter responds with an HTTP 429 status and a **`Retry-After`** header, as shown above. This signals to browsers and well-behaved clients how many seconds to wait before retrying. Many HTTP libraries and browsers respect this header, backing off automatically and reducing server strain.

You can also add custom headers (**`X-RateLimit-Limit`**, **`X-RateLimit-Remaining`**, etc.) for further transparency:

```
from fastapi.responses import JSONResponse
@router.get("/user-resource")
async def user_resource(request: Request, user_id: int = 123):
    await sliding_window_rate_limit(request, user_id=user_id,
limit=10, window_seconds=60)
    # Calculate current remaining requests if you want to show
    redis = await get_redis()
```

```
    key = get_rate_limit_key(request, user_id, "sliding")
    count = await redis.zcard(key)
    remaining = max(0, 10 - count)
    headers = {
        "X-RateLimit-Limit": "10",
        "X-RateLimit-Remaining": str(remaining)
    }
    return JSONResponse({"msg": "User resource accessed."},
headers=headers)
```

Now that we've got these safeguards set up, we're all set to prevent misuse, accidental DDoS, and runaway scripts. You can:

- Test using automated tools, scripts, or even browser tabs.
- Tune the limits and windows per endpoint based on real-world usage.
- Combine different algorithms for different endpoints (e.g., fixed for public APIs, sliding for sensitive or paid routes).
- Log excessive usage for audit or alerting.
- Adapt keys to support API keys, session IDs, or device fingerprints for even more granularity.

These patterns are ready for immediate production use and can be adapted or expanded to meet any advanced need as our system evolves.

Background Task Queues

The more complex our app becomes, the more workloads like generating PDF reports, exporting large datasets, running database cleanups, or sending batch notifications can't be done with an HTTP request. When you've got long-running tasks, they can block user requests, use up worker resources, and make the API feel unresponsive. If you delegate heavy or slow jobs to a background task queue, you'll keep the application snappy, handle workload spikes gracefully, and enable automation that runs on its own schedule.

Together, celery and Redis make a solid background processing stack that's been tested and proven in production. Now, we're going to add more job types and set up multi-step workflows with callback chains. This will be the foundation for automated, scalable backend processing.

Celery with Redis as Broker and Result Backend

Redis is a natural broker for Celery in modern Python projects. To avoid redundant setup, we rely on our prior configuration, but we will make the connections explicit and reusable for report, cleanup, and other jobs.

```
# app/celery_worker.py
from celery import Celery
import os
REDIS_URL = os.getenv("REDIS_URL", "redis://localhost:6379/0")
celery_app = Celery(
    "myapp_tasks",
    broker=REDIS_URL,
    backend=REDIS_URL
)
# For code organization, we import task modules here so Celery knows about them.
import app.tasks
```

All Celery workers and our web app should point to the same Redis instance (or cluster). This ensures jobs flow smoothly between producers (the web/API) and consumers (workers).

Background Tasks for Report Generation and Cleanup Jobs

Report Generation Task

There are various reports, like sales summaries, analytics, or invoice PDFs, which often require heavy database queries and significant processing. We can simply offload these to Celery as shown below:

```
# app/tasks.py
from app.celery_worker import celery_app
import time
import random
@celery_app.task(bind=True)
def generate_report_task(self, report_id, user_id):
    # Simulate time-intensive processing
    time.sleep(random.randint(5, 10))
```

```
    # Example result: Save or update DB (omitted for brevity)
    result = {"report_id": report_id, "status": "ready",
"url": f"/reports/{report_id}.pdf"}
    print(f"Report for {user_id} generated: {result['url']}")
    return result
```

This job might be triggered by a user action or a scheduled workflow. On completion, it could notify the user or update a database status.

Cleanup Task

In addition, we can also do regular cleanup things like removing old sessions, deleting expired data, or compacting logs. Here too, the Celery is ideal for scheduling or manually triggering such jobs:

```
@celery_app.task(bind=True)
def cleanup_expired_sessions_task(self):
    print("Cleanup started: expired sessions.")
    time.sleep(3)  # Simulate cleanup duration
    print("Cleanup finished: expired sessions.")
    return {"status": "cleanup_complete"}
```

These jobs are typically scheduled with Celery's periodic tasks, but can also be chained after certain triggers.

Triggering Tasks from FastAPI Endpoints

We can also integrate background jobs seamlessly into our app by triggering them as needed:

```
# app/routes/admin.py
from fastapi import APIRouter
from app.tasks import generate_report_task,
cleanup_expired_sessions_task
router = APIRouter()
@router.post("/reports/generate")
def generate_report(user_id: int):
    report_id = random.randint(1000, 9999)
```

```
    task = generate_report_task.delay(report_id, user_id)
    return {"msg": "Report generation started", "task_id":
task.id}
@router.post("/admin/cleanup")
def cleanup_sessions():
    task = cleanup_expired_sessions_task.delay()
    return {"msg": "Cleanup started", "task_id": task.id}
```

The users or admins get instant feedback that the job has started, while the actual heavy work happens asynchronously.

Chaining Tasks with Callback Workflows

There are complex automations that often need to chain several jobs in sequence or in parallel, such as generating a report, then emailing the user, and finally logging the outcome. We can do it using Celery as it provides powerful primitives as below:

Using Chains

A ***chain*** ensures one task runs after another, passing results along:

```
from celery import chain
@celery_app.task
def notify_user_task(result, user_id):
    print(f"Notify user {user_id}: report is ready at
{result['url']}")
    # In a real app, send email/SMS notification
    return {"notified": True}
# Trigger a chain: generate report -> notify user
def start_report_workflow(report_id, user_id):
    job_chain = chain(
        generate_report_task.s(report_id, user_id),
        notify_user_task.s(user_id)
    )
    job_chain.apply_async()
```

The **.s** method ("signature") prepares arguments. Results flow from one task to the next, ensuring reliable, ordered processing.

Using Callbacks with 'link'

For simpler cases, you can attach a callback with **link**:

```
task = generate_report_task.apply_async((report_id, user_id),
link=notify_user_task.s(user_id))
```

When **generate_report_task** finishes, **notify_user_task** runs with its result and the extra argument.

Parallel Workflows and Groups

The Celery also supports running groups of tasks in parallel, which can be useful for cleanup jobs spanning multiple datasets:

```
from celery import group
def run_cleanup_jobs():
    cleanup_group = group(
        cleanup_expired_sessions_task.s(),
        # Add other cleanup tasks as needed
    )
    cleanup_group.apply_async()
```

Here, the results are collected when all parallel jobs finish.

Monitoring Background Task Queues

You can observe and manage all these jobs using the Flower tool, as covered previously. This real-time dashboard shows running, successful, failed, or pending jobs, thereby making troubleshooting and performance tuning straightforward.

- ***Retries***: If a task fails (due to a database outage, for instance), Celery can automatically retry it, or escalate to alerts.
- ***Timeouts***: Configure timeouts or maximum runtime to prevent jobs from hanging indefinitely.
- ***Crontab Scheduling***: Celery Beat allows periodic jobs (e.g., cleanup every night at midnight).

AsyncIO Endpoints

Whenever we build features that reach out to databases, remote APIs, or file storage, we run into a familiar challenge: parts of our code have to wait for someone else. In a classic synchronous application, our server pauses the moment it hits a slow database or an external service, other users keep stacking up behind, each waiting for their turn. This setup can be fine for simple workloads, but as soon as we grow or need to connect to more systems, it starts holding us back.

We'll look closely at how we can migrate our FastAPI routes to async, and then see firsthand the power of running dozens of outbound calls at once with HTTPX, all while using clean, readable code that's a pleasure to maintain.

ASYNC Patterns

The async programming in Python centers around two keywords: **async** and **await**. When we define a function with **async def**, it becomes a coroutine, a function that can "give up" the thread whenever it's waiting, letting the event loop run other work. By placing **await** in front of an I/O operation (like a database call or an HTTP request), we tell Python, "Go ahead and handle other things until this operation is ready."

For our FastAPI application, we can mix async and regular routes freely. Async endpoints shine when we're dealing with lots of I/O like, calling APIs, fetching files, or streaming data. Each async route leaves the server free to process more requests, instead of tying up threads in limbo.

Converting FastAPI Routes to Async Functions

So here, let us assume that we started with a synchronous route like this:

```
@router.get("/slow-profile/{user_id}")
def get_profile(user_id: int):
    profile = slow_db_query(user_id)  # Blocking: all other
requests must wait
    return profile
```

Whenever a request comes in, our worker waits for the database, serving nothing else until it's done. But if our database driver supports async, we can write:

```
@router.get("/profile/{user_id}")
async def get_profile(user_id: int):
    profile = await async_db_query(user_id)  # Non-blocking:
serves other users during wait
```

```
    return profile
```

Now, as soon as **async_db_query** starts waiting, FastAPI moves on, letting other requests be handled. The change is subtle in code but huge in effect, especially under high load.

Running Multiple HTTP Calls

Let's say we need to combine several external APIs—user details, stats, maybe a recommendation engine. If we call them one after the other, we add up all their latencies. But with HTTPX's **AsyncClient**, we can fire them all off together, then wait for all to finish in a single shot.

Following is how we might approach this, step by step:

1. Define our route as **async def**.
2. Create an async HTTPX client.
3. Start all the calls using **client.get(...)**, but don't **await** them yet.
4. Use **await asyncio.gather(...)** to pause until all are ready.
5. Assemble the results and return.

The given below is the sample code program:

```
import httpx
import asyncio
from fastapi import APIRouter
router = APIRouter()
@router.get("/aggregate/{user_id}")
async def aggregate_user_data(user_id: int):
    user_url = f"https://api.example.com/users/{user_id}"
    stats_url = f"https://api.example.com/stats/{user_id}"
    rec_url = f"https://api.example.com/recs/{user_id}"
    async with httpx.AsyncClient() as client:
        # We start all requests right away
        user_future = client.get(user_url)
        stats_future = client.get(stats_url)
        rec_future = client.get(rec_url)
        # Then we pause until all are complete
```

```
        user_resp, stats_resp, rec_resp = await
asyncio.gather(user_future, stats_future, rec_future)
        # Parse each result
        user_data = user_resp.json()
        stats_data = stats_resp.json()
        recs_data = rec_resp.json()
    return {
        "user": user_data,
        "stats": stats_data,
        "recommendations": recs_data
    }
```

In this way, we turn three slow calls into one fast group. The time it takes is only as long as the slowest single request—never the sum of all.

Streaming Data and File Responses

With async, we can also efficiently serve large files or data streams to users, letting them start downloading as soon as possible while keeping memory usage low. Suppose we want to offer file downloads, even while many users are active, and if we create a async generator, we can read and send out file chunks one by one as shown below:

```
import aiofiles
from fastapi.responses import StreamingResponse
@router.get("/download/{file_id}")
async def download_file(file_id: str):
    async def file_streamer():
        async with aiofiles.open(f"files/{file_id}.dat",
mode='rb') as f:
            while True:
                chunk = await f.read(64 * 1024)  # Read in
64KB chunks
                if not chunk:
                    break
```

```
                yield chunk
    return StreamingResponse(file_streamer(),
media_type="application/octet-stream")
```

In the above, our server starts sending the file as soon as the first chunk is ready, all while still serving other users without bottlenecks.

Handling Timeouts, Errors, and Resource Cleanup

The async codes also means thinking a bit differently about errors and timeouts. When we reach out to third-party APIs, we always want to protect ourselves from hanging forever. Here, the HTTPX lets us specify timeouts and handle failures gracefully:

```
@router.get("/external-check")
async def external_check():
    try:
        async with httpx.AsyncClient(timeout=4.0) as client:
            resp = await
client.get("https://api.slowpartner.com/data")
            resp.raise_for_status()
            return resp.json()
    except httpx.TimeoutException:
        return {"error": "External service timed out."}
    except httpx.HTTPStatusError as exc:
        return {"error": f"Remote error:
{exc.response.status_code}"}
```

So, by catching exceptions, we keep our users informed and our app robust, even if a remote service is slow or unavailable. When we test our endpoints with multiple clients, the difference is striking: rather than piling up in a backlog, requests are processed in parallel, so users wait less and see more immediate results.

Summary

To wrap things up, we made our app faster and more reliable as more people started using it and the demands increased. We started by setting up Redis-backed caching, using it for both function-level and route-level responses to minimize latency and offload repetitive computation. We also figured out TTL values and cache invalidation patterns so that data stayed fresh without sacrificing performance. We then added things like rate limiting and throttling, tracked each user's or IP's activity in Redis, and used both fixed window and sliding window algorithms to make sure everyone was using things fairly and protect our resources. And we made sure to always include clear Retry-After headers to guide client behavior.

As our workflows got more complicated, we set up Celery and Redis together as a solid background task queue, creating reliable jobs for reporting, cleanup, and chaining callbacks to automate entire business processes. We finally decided to go with Python's async features in FastAPI. We changed some of the key endpoints to async and used HTTPX to run multiple outbound calls at the same time. This showed how using concurrent I/O can make the whole system more responsive and scalable.

CHAPTER 6: DATA PROCESSING UTILITIES

Overview

This chapter will show you how to set the app up with useful tools for working with and changing all the most important types of business data. First you'll learn how to read and write CSV and Excel files fast—even when the files are huge. You'll learn how to use streaming approaches that save memory and make the most of your computer's power. Then, it'll show you how to use Jinja2 templates for dynamic content and WeasyPrint or headless Chrome to create professional documents that get sent straight to clients through asynchronous endpoints. You'll learn how to resize, generate, and store derivatives for any upload scenario with Pillow, and you'll develop strategies to handle common pitfalls along the way.

Finally, you'll learn about Markdown-to-HTML conversion, which lets you process user content safely and sanitize HTML output to protect against XSS attacks. You'll also learn to embed the results smoothly into Jinja2 templates. By the time you're done with this chapter, you'll have a bunch of data processing tools that'll keep the app fast, secure, and adaptable. That way, it'll be able to handle the real-world needs of our users and business partners.

CSV & Excel Parsing

Basically, any data-driven stuff you've got, whether it's for analytics, integration, or migration, it needs to be able to handle tabular data at some point. You'll find spreadsheets are used pretty much everywhere in business reporting, legacy systems, and even modern APIs that need to support human-friendly data interchange. But, putting files into memory is only good for small amounts of data. As our files get bigger, like tens or hundreds of megabytes, we need a better plan that balances speed, memory use, and reliability.

With the right tools, like Python's libraries, we can handle pretty much anything. For this topic, we'll stick with just the core and widely adopted libraries (**`csv`** and **`openpyxl`**), keeping our environment simple, dependencies minimal, and workflows portable across platforms.

Streaming Large CSV Files with 'csv'

The **`csv`** module in Python's standard library provides an efficient and highly flexible way to handle CSVs. By opening files in text mode and reading line by line, we avoid loading the entire file into memory—essential when working with large datasets.

Suppose we receive a file, **`large_dataset.csv`**, that has millions of rows. We want to process each row for analytics, import, or filtering. Following is how we set up a streaming read:

```
import csv
def process_large_csv(file_path):
```

```
    with open(file_path, mode='r', encoding='utf-8',
newline='') as f:
        reader = csv.DictReader(f)
        for row in reader:
            # Process each row: print, validate, or accumulate
as needed
            handle_row(row)
```

By using **DictReader**, we automatically map columns to keys, so each **row** becomes a dictionary. The file is never fully loaded into memory; instead, each line is processed in a steady, predictable manner, no matter how large the input.

For example, if we want to filter and write only certain rows to a new file, we can chain this logic directly:

```
def filter_and_export_csv(input_path, output_path,
filter_func):
    with open(input_path, mode='r', encoding='utf-8',
newline='') as infile, \
         open(output_path, mode='w', encoding='utf-8',
newline='') as outfile:
        reader = csv.DictReader(infile)
        writer = csv.DictWriter(outfile,
fieldnames=reader.fieldnames)
        writer.writeheader()
        for row in reader:
            if filter_func(row):
                writer.writerow(row)
```

This function reads from the source, applies a filter, and writes only selected records to the destination, all in a streaming, memory-efficient fashion.

Exporting Data as CSV

Sometimes, we need to generate CSVs for reports or data exchange, possibly from database queries or computed data. We make sure our writes are streamlined, so they don't take up much memory and work well with other tools as shown below:

```
def export_data_to_csv(rows, output_path, fieldnames):
    with open(output_path, mode='w', encoding='utf-8',
newline='') as f:
        writer = csv.DictWriter(f, fieldnames=fieldnames)
        writer.writeheader()
        for row in rows:
            writer.writerow(row)
```

In the above, **rows** can be any iterable, even a generator yielding thousands of rows. This makes the function suitable for live data exports, such as serving downloads directly to the user in a web application.

Reading Large Excel Files with 'openpyxl'

Unlike CSVs, the Excel files are more complex. They support multiple sheets, cell formatting, and various encodings. The **openpyxl** is the gold standard for **.xlsx** files in Python, allowing both random access and streaming reads. For massive Excel files, we want to avoid loading the full workbook into memory. **openpyxl** provides a "read-only" mode that streams row by row.

Given below is how we open and iterate through a large file:

```
from openpyxl import load_workbook
def process_large_excel(file_path, sheet_name=None):
    wb = load_workbook(file_path, read_only=True,
data_only=True)
    ws = wb[sheet_name] if sheet_name else wb.active
    for row in ws.iter_rows(values_only=True):
        handle_row(row)
```

In **read_only** mode, only a small portion of the file is held in memory at any moment. The **values_only** flag ensures we get just the cell contents, not formatting objects, streamlining our processing even further.

If we need column headers, we can extract the first row and map subsequent rows to dicts:

```
def process_excel_with_headers(file_path, sheet_name=None):
    wb = load_workbook(file_path, read_only=True,
data_only=True)
```

```
    ws = wb[sheet_name] if sheet_name else wb.active
    rows = ws.iter_rows(values_only=True)
    headers = next(rows)
    for values in rows:
        row = dict(zip(headers, values))
        handle_row(row)
```

This makes Excel processing as comfortable as CSV, while still respecting the file's native structure.

Writing and Exporting Excel Files

Now here, to generate reports or share processed data, we often need to write data back to Excel. With **openpyxl**, we can create new files, add sheets, and stream rows to disk.

```
from openpyxl import Workbook
def export_data_to_excel(rows, output_path, headers):
    wb = Workbook(write_only=True)
    ws = wb.create_sheet()
    ws.append(headers)
    for row in rows:
        ws.append([row.get(header, "") for header in headers])
    wb.save(output_path)
```

By using **write_only=True**, we tell **openpyxl** to avoid holding the entire workbook in memory. This is critical for exports involving tens or hundreds of thousands of rows.

Handling Encodings, Data Types, and Errors

Both CSV and Excel files can present edge cases—mismatched encodings, inconsistent column counts, or mixed data types. To keep our scripts robust, we:

- Explicitly set encoding (**utf-8** is safest for most modern files).
- Validate each row, catching and logging exceptions without breaking the stream.
- Handle missing or extra columns by using dict **.get()** and default values.
- Normalize data types as early as possible (e.g., convert numeric strings to numbers).

Following is a simple example of error handling in a streaming context:

```
def safe_handle_row(row):
    try:
        # Custom validation or conversion logic
        process_row(row)
    except Exception as e:
        log_error(e, row)
```

By adopting streaming reads and writes, our scripts can handle datasets that would crash conventional in-memory approaches. We can process gigabyte-scale files on machines with modest resources, making our utilities suitable for everything from quick ETL pipelines to production web services. Throughout this topic, we have developed a toolkit for working confidently with CSV and Excel data like parsing, filtering, and exporting massive files with efficiency and reliability, using only Python's best-supported libraries. These patterns will become the backbone for any kind of large-scale data processing that our application will face, now or in the future.

PDF Report Generation

The ability to generate professional, automated PDF reports is a key feature for any data-driven application, whether it's for billing, analytics, compliance, or client-facing summaries. They're universally readable, print-ready, and can have rich styling via HTML/CSS, so they're the go-to output format for invoices and custom analytics dashboards.

Rather than building PDFs from scratch, we can rely on modern tools that turn HTML (with all its layout and design capabilities) into pixel-perfect, standards-compliant PDFs. The two best choices for this in Python are ***WeasyPrint***, a pure Python, CSS-compliant renderer, and ***headless Chrome***, which brings full browser rendering power to server-side scripts. Both can be integrated cleanly with Jinja2, letting us fill templates with live data and instantly deliver beautiful reports.

Creating Jinja2-Based HTML Templates

Now here, our first goal is to build HTML templates for our reports, using Jinja2 for dynamic content. Jinja2 is the same templating engine we already use for web pages and emails, so we have a unified workflow for all templated output.

Suppose we want a report showing transaction details, summary stats, and a custom header. We start by creating a template file, such as **`templates/report.html`**:

```
<!DOCTYPE html>
<html lang="en">
```

```
<head>
    <meta charset="UTF-8">
    <title>{{ report_title }}</title>
    <style>
        body { font-family: 'DejaVu Sans', sans-serif; margin:
24px; color: #222; }
        h1, h2 { border-bottom: 1px solid #ddd; }
        table { width: 100%; border-collapse: collapse;
margin-top: 18px; }
        th, td { border: 1px solid #bbb; padding: 8px 12px;
text-align: left; }
        th { background: #f7f7f7; }
        .summary { margin-top: 22px; font-size: 1.08em; }
    </style>
</head>
<body>
    <h1>{{ report_title }}</h1>
    <div class="summary">
        <p>Generated at: {{ generated_at }}</p>
        <p>Total Transactions: {{ transactions | length }}</p>
        <p>Report Author: {{ author }}</p>
    </div>
    <h2>Transaction Details</h2>
    <table>
        <thead>
            <tr>

<th>Date</th><th>Description</th><th>Amount</th>
            </tr>
        </thead>
        <tbody>
```

```
            {% for t in transactions %}
            <tr>
                <td>{{ t.date }}</td>
                <td>{{ t.description }}</td>
                <td style="text-align:right;">{{
"%.2f"|format(t.amount) }}</td>
            </tr>
            {% endfor %}
        </tbody>
    </table>
</body>
</html>
```

This template provides a foundation that we can reuse for any data structure. By passing different variables, we can create anything from summaries to detailed logs.

Rendering HTML with Jinja2

When we use the template, we render it from Python and supply the variables needed for the report. We'll set up a utility for that:

```
from jinja2 import Environment, FileSystemLoader
from datetime import datetime
def render_report_html(transactions, author="System",
title="Transaction Report"):
    env = Environment(loader=FileSystemLoader("templates"))
    template = env.get_template("report.html")
    html = template.render(
        report_title=title,
        generated_at=datetime.utcnow().strftime("%Y-%m-%d
%H:%M UTC"),
        author=author,
        transactions=transactions
    )
```

```
    return html
```

In the above, **transactions** are a list of dicts, each representing a transaction. The function returns a complete HTML string, ready for PDF conversion.

Rendering HTML to PDF using WeasyPrint

As said earlier, the WeasyPrint is a pure Python solution for converting HTML and CSS to PDF. It supports much of the CSS standard and is reliable for most business-style reports. To get started, let us first get it installed:

```
pip install weasyprint
```

Now, we then convert the rendered HTML to PDF:

```
from weasyprint import HTML
def html_to_pdf_bytes(html: str) -> bytes:
    pdf_file = HTML(string=html).write_pdf()
    return pdf_file
```

This function takes HTML as input and returns the PDF as a bytes object, ready to save or stream. This technique works well for both small and large reports and does not require launching a browser.

Serving PDFs via Asynchronous Streaming Endpoints

To deliver these reports efficiently, we want to stream PDFs directly to the client, letting them start the download instantly, while keeping our server's memory use and thread count minimal. The FastAPI's **StreamingResponse** lets us do this naturally with async endpoints.

Following is a complete example:

```
from fastapi import APIRouter, Response
from fastapi.responses import StreamingResponse
import io
router = APIRouter()
@router.post("/reports/pdf")
async def generate_pdf_report(data: dict):
    transactions = data.get("transactions", [])
```

```
    author = data.get("author", "System")
    title = data.get("title", "Transaction Report")
    # stage 1: Render HTML
    html = render_report_html(transactions, author, title)
    # stage 2: Render PDF (sync or async)
    pdf_bytes = html_to_pdf_bytes(html)  # WeasyPrint version
    # stage 3: Stream PDF as response
    return StreamingResponse(io.BytesIO(pdf_bytes),
media_type="application/pdf", headers={
        "Content-Disposition": "inline; filename=report.pdf"
    })
```

If you are using headless Chrome, wrap our call with **await** and adapt the endpoint to async (since Playwright is fully async):

```
@router.post("/reports/pdf-chrome")
async def generate_pdf_report_chrome(data: dict):
    transactions = data.get("transactions", [])
    author = data.get("author", "System")
    title = data.get("title", "Transaction Report")
    html = render_report_html(transactions, author, title)
    pdf_bytes = await html_to_pdf_with_chrome(html)
    return StreamingResponse(io.BytesIO(pdf_bytes),
media_type="application/pdf", headers={
        "Content-Disposition": "inline; filename=report.pdf"
    })
```

For truly massive reports, you can render content in sections, flush output in chunks, or use temporary files as buffers. The FastAPI and Python's **io** modules are flexible enough to support any scale.

Throughout this topic, we have woven together the essential techniques for building PDF reports in Python applications: templating, high-quality rendering, and non-blocking delivery. These skills let us create polished, flexible documents for every business scenario, all from a familiar, maintainable codebase.

Image Thumbnailing

Any app that handles uploads of images, like for avatars, galleries, product listings, or reports, needs to generate thumbnails. With thumbnails, you can quickly and easily see images at the right size for any device or screen. We keep our UI fast and save bandwidth for users by storing pre-generated, appropriately-sized thumbnails. This also means we can offer responsive layouts or retina-ready images without overburdening the backend.

But luckily, Python's Pillow library makes it a breeze. It's got all the tools we need to make these image transformations, and it supports all the major formats. Plus, it's a well-tested API, so you can count on it. In the next few sections, we'll look at how to add Pillow to our stack, integrate it with FastAPI endpoints, generate multiple thumbnail sizes, and design solid error handling for this image workflow.

Installing Pillow

First, we will ensure Pillow is installed in our environment:

```
pip install pillow
```

Pillow is lightweight but powerful, supporting everything from simple resizing to advanced color transformations and metadata preservation. Once installed, we can import it and use its Image class for all our image manipulation tasks.

Building Image Upload and Thumbnailing Endpoint

Suppose our app allows users to upload images. We want to process each upload as follows:

1. Save the original image.
2. Generate several thumbnail sizes (say, 64x64, 128x128, 256x256 pixels).
3. Store all derivatives in a clear, predictable folder structure for easy access later.

We will walk through a practical implementation. First, here's a basic FastAPI route for uploads:

```
from fastapi import APIRouter, UploadFile, File, HTTPException
from PIL import Image
import os
router = APIRouter()
UPLOAD_DIR = "uploaded_images"
THUMBNAIL_SIZES = [(64, 64), (128, 128), (256, 256)]
os.makedirs(UPLOAD_DIR, exist_ok=True)
```

```
@router.post("/upload-image/")
async def upload_image(file: UploadFile = File(...)):
    if not file.content_type.startswith("image/"):
        raise HTTPException(status_code=400, detail="Invalid
image format")
    file_ext = os.path.splitext(file.filename)[1].lower()
    save_path = os.path.join(UPLOAD_DIR, file.filename)
    # Save original file
    with open(save_path, "wb") as out_file:
        content = await file.read()
        out_file.write(content)
    # Generate and save thumbnails
    thumbnails = []
    try:
        image = Image.open(save_path)
        for size in THUMBNAIL_SIZES:
            thumb = image.copy()
            thumb.thumbnail(size)
            thumb_name =
f"{os.path.splitext(file.filename)[0]}_{size[0]}x{size[1]}{fil
e_ext}"
            thumb_path = os.path.join(UPLOAD_DIR, thumb_name)
            thumb.save(thumb_path)
            thumbnails.append({"size": size, "path":
thumb_path})
    except Exception as e:
        raise HTTPException(status_code=500, detail=f"Image
processing failed: {e}")
    return {
        "original": save_path,
        "thumbnails": thumbnails
```

```
}
```

In this route:

- We check that the file is an image by checking its content type.
- We save the original image in our upload directory.
- For each desired size, we create a thumbnail using Pillow's **`thumbnail()`** method, save it with a distinct name, and keep a record of its location.

Generating Multiple Thumbnail Dimensions in One Pass

The Pillow **`thumbnail()`** method maintains the image's aspect ratio, fitting it into the given box. By copying the original image before resizing, we ensure each thumbnail is crisp and avoids cumulative quality loss. We can easily expand the **`THUMBNAIL_SIZES`** list to support any number of responsive or retina-ready formats.

If you want thumbnails with exact dimensions (cropping instead of just resizing), you can add a utility to crop the center square after resizing, but in most use-cases, standard thumbnails suffice for performance and simplicity.

Markdown-to-HTML Conversion

The Markdown has become the de facto way for users to write formatted content in everything from blog posts and product descriptions to comments and internal documentation. It offers a simple, human-friendly syntax while still supporting all the common structures people need—headings, lists, code blocks, and links. The main challenge comes in safely converting this user-written Markdown to HTML for rendering in web pages, since direct conversion without security checks can allow XSS attacks or layout issues.

For this task, the **`markdown-it-py`** library provides fast, extensible Markdown parsing, closely mirroring the popular JS implementation. And, by combining it with a sanitizer such as **`bleach`**, we gain confidence that user-generated HTML won't introduce vulnerabilities.

Installing 'markdown-it-py' and 'bleach'

Before we start, we will ensure our environment includes both **`markdown-it-py`** for parsing and **`bleach`** for sanitizing:

```
pip install markdown-it-py bleach
```

Both packages are lightweight and have no impact on the rest of our stack. **`markdown-it-py`** offers a rich parsing experience, while **`bleach`** gives us granular control over which HTML tags and attributes are allowed.

Parsing Markdown Content

The core workflow is straightforward: we take the raw Markdown input (for example, from a user's comment or article), feed it into the Markdown parser, and obtain HTML.

Following is a practical function for this transformation:

```
from markdown_it import MarkdownIt
def markdown_to_html(markdown_text: str) -> str:
    md = MarkdownIt()
    html = md.render(markdown_text)
    return html
```

This function can be reused across endpoints and templates, making it easy to convert content on demand.

Sanitizing HTML Output to Prevent XSS

Markdown conversion can generate HTML tags, but some tags (like **`<script>`**, **`<iframe>`**, or even inline event handlers) can be abused. To prevent XSS, we sanitize the HTML before passing it to templates.

Here, the **`bleach`** lets us specify exactly which tags and attributes are allowed. Given below is how we wrap the conversion:

```
import bleach
ALLOWED_TAGS = [
    'a', 'abbr', 'acronym', 'b', 'blockquote', 'code', 'em',
'i',
    'li', 'ol', 'ul', 'strong', 'pre', 'p', 'br', 'h1', 'h2',
'h3', 'h4', 'h5', 'h6'
]
ALLOWED_ATTRS = {
    'a': ['href', 'title', 'rel'],
    'abbr': ['title'],
    'acronym': ['title'],
}
def sanitize_html(unsafe_html: str) -> str:
```

```
    return bleach.clean(
        unsafe_html,
        tags=ALLOWED_TAGS,
        attributes=ALLOWED_ATTRS,
        strip=True
    )
```

If we combine both the functions, we can get a secure Markdown rendering utility:

```
def render_markdown_safe(markdown_text: str) -> str:
    html = markdown_to_html(markdown_text)
    safe_html = sanitize_html(html)
    return safe_html
```

This ensures that no user-supplied Markdown can break out of the content area or execute unwanted scripts.

Embedding Rendered HTML in Jinja2

Now, we will see how to present Markdown content in our application's web views. Suppose we have a FastAPI route that receives or loads Markdown data and needs to display it in a template.

Following is a pattern for rendering a Markdown-powered blog post or comment:

```
from fastapi import APIRouter, Request
from fastapi.templating import Jinja2Templates
router = APIRouter()
templates = Jinja2Templates(directory="templates")
@router.get("/article/{article_id}")
async def show_article(request: Request, article_id: int):
    # Imagine we load markdown_content from a database
    markdown_content = load_markdown_from_db(article_id)
    rendered_html = render_markdown_safe(markdown_content)
    return templates.TemplateResponse(
        "article.html",
```

```
        {"request": request, "article_html": rendered_html}
    )
```

In our Jinja2 template, we embed the HTML directly. To prevent auto-escaping (which would turn tags back into plain text), we then make use of the **|safe** filter:

```
<!-- templates/article.html -->
<!DOCTYPE html>
<html>
<head>
    <title>Article</title>
</head>
<body>
    <article>
        {{ article_html | safe }}
    </article>
</body>
</html>
```

This pattern keeps everything modular, reusable, and secure. Any time we want to display Markdown, from profile bios to support tickets, we can use this workflow. With these techniques, we have created a complete Markdown-to-HTML utility for our application which is reliable for users, and safe for our infrastructure. This toolchain can power blogs, wikis, product reviews, and any other rich-text experience we want to offer, while keeping our development workflow efficient and maintainable.

Summary

To sum it up, we came up with a solid set of tools for handling all sorts of data processing needs that are common these days. We started by working through the details of parsing large CSV and Excel files. We used efficient streaming patterns with Python's built-in csv module and openpyxl to make sure even the largest datasets could be processed or exported without memory issues. Then, we started using PDF reports, designing dynamic Jinja2 templates for our data and rendering them to polished PDFs with WeasyPrint or a headless Chrome browser. All of this was done while delivering these files directly to users via non-blocking, asynchronous endpoints.

We expanded our workflow to include image thumbnailing, using Pillow to resize and generate multiple thumbnail dimensions for uploaded images. We also discussed strategies for reliable storage and addressed preprocessing challenges like corrupt files or naming conflicts. We wrapped up the chapter by setting up a Markdown-to-HTML conversion pipeline that combines markdown-it-py with bleach for secure, flexible content formatting, and showed how to embed sanitized HTML safely in our Jinja2 templates. We made some patterns through each utility that put performance, reliability, and security first. This makes sure that our application stays efficient and easy to use, even as it grows.

Chapter 7: Deployment & Operations

Overview

Today, we're going to look at how to take our Python application from local development to robust, production-grade operations using today's most reliable DevOps tools and patterns. You'll start by getting a handle on Docker Compose, learning how to describe, configure, and launch all the supporting services such as, database, cache, and brokers, and all this using a single, version-controlled configuration. Then, we'll dive into building efficient, multi-stage Docker images to make deployments faster and more secure. You'll learn to implement centralized log aggregation with the ELK stack, configure Filebeat to ship rich, structured logs, design real-time Kibana dashboards, and set up alerts that help our team respond instantly to operational issues.

As our apps grow beyond the capacity of a single host, you'll start diving into Kubernetes, writing manifests to define how things are deployed, what services are provided, and how traffic is routed. You'll also be the one in charge of keeping everything updated and making sure everything goes smoothly with **`kubectl`**. By the time you're done with this chapter, you'll have the tools and hands-on experience you need to confidently deploy, monitor, and manage scalable apps. This means every change is predictable, every outage is visible, and every deployment is repeatable and safe.

Docker & Docker Compose

A robust deployment isn't just "the app". It's the app, the database, the cache layer, perhaps a message broker, and sometimes background workers or even frontend assets. Managing this tangle of services by hand is a recipe for confusion, version drift, and lost productivity. This is where ***Docker Compose*** steps in, letting us describe and control every part of our operational stack with a single file.

The Docker Compose lets us define, configure, and run multi-container Docker applications using simple YAML. Each service is described with its build or image, environment variables, ports, volumes, and dependencies. With a single command, we spin up every component, always with the exact versions and settings we expect, whether for development, testing, or production. The Compose even supports lifecycle management (start, stop, restart), networking between services, and one-off commands for migrations or data loading. In effect, it provides us with a portable, repeatable, and shareable deployment blueprint.

Setting up Docker Compose

Before we can orchestrate, we need Docker and Docker Compose available. Most modern Docker installations include Compose, but for completeness, following is the setup:

Install Docker

At first, just download and install the Docker Desktop or the Docker Engine package.

```
docker compose version
```

If you see a version number, you're set. If not, update our Docker installation.

Project Layout

For our project, we organize our root directory like this:

```
.
├── app/
│   └── main.py
├── requirements.txt
├── Dockerfile
├── docker-compose.yml
├── .env
```

Here, the:

- **app/** holds our FastAPI code.
- **requirements.txt** lists our dependencies.
- **Dockerfile** defines how we build our app image.
- **docker-compose.yml** configures all containers and services.
- **.env** holds sensitive or environment-specific variables (never committed to version control).

Optimized Multi-Stage Dockerfile

The multi-stage Dockerfiles let us separate the build and runtime environments, producing minimal, secure, and efficient images. For Python apps, this means no build tools or test dependencies are shipped in production, and the final image stays lean.

We will build one step by step:

```
# Dockerfile
# Stage 1: Build dependencies
FROM python:3.11-slim AS builder
```

```
WORKDIR /build
# System deps for psycopg2, pillow, etc.
RUN apt-get update && apt-get install -y --no-install-
recommends \
    gcc \
    libpq-dev \
    build-essential \
    && rm -rf /var/lib/apt/lists/*
COPY requirements.txt .
RUN pip install --upgrade pip && pip wheel --no-cache-dir --
wheel-dir /wheels -r requirements.txt
# Stage 2: Minimal runtime
FROM python:3.11-slim
WORKDIR /app
# System deps for runtime
RUN apt-get update && apt-get install -y --no-install-
recommends \
    libpq-dev \
    && rm -rf /var/lib/apt/lists/*
COPY --from=builder /wheels /wheels
COPY --from=builder /build/requirements.txt .
RUN pip install --no-cache-dir --find-links=/wheels -r
requirements.txt
COPY app/ /app/
# Add a non-root user for security
RUN useradd -m appuser
USER appuser
CMD ["uvicorn", "main:app", "--host", "0.0.0.0", "--port",
"8000"]
```

In the above,

- The ***builder*** stage compiles and wheels dependencies, including any native code.

- The final image contains only what's needed to run—no build tools, just wheels and source.
- **useradd** ensures our process does not run as root.
- The command uses Uvicorn, but this can be adjusted for any WSGI/ASGI server.

Configuring 'docker-compose.yml' for Full Stack

Our application rarely stands alone; it likely relies on a database (e.g., Postgres), a cache (Redis), and a broker (such as Redis again for Celery or RabbitMQ). The Compose lets us declare all these services, their environment, and their connectivity.

So here, we will design a practical **docker-compose.yml**:

```
version: "3.9"
services:
  web:
    build: .
    command: uvicorn main:app --host 0.0.0.0 --port 8000 --
reload
    volumes:
      - ./app:/app
    env_file:
      - .env
    ports:
      - "8000:8000"
    depends_on:
      - db
      - redis
    environment:
      -
DATABASE_URL=postgresql://postgres:postgres@db:5432/postgres
      - REDIS_URL=redis://redis:6379/0
  db:
    image: postgres:15
```

```
    restart: always
    environment:
      POSTGRES_DB: postgres
      POSTGRES_USER: postgres
      POSTGRES_PASSWORD: postgres
    ports:
      - "5432:5432"
    volumes:
      - pgdata:/var/lib/postgresql/data
  redis:
    image: redis:7
    restart: always
    ports:
      - "6379:6379"
    volumes:
      - redisdata:/data
  celery:
    build: .
    command: celery -A app.celery_worker.celery_app worker --
loglevel=info
    env_file:
      - .env
    depends_on:
      - web
      - redis
  flower:
    image: mher/flower
    command: flower --broker=redis://redis:6379/0
    ports:
      - "5555:5555"
```

```
    depends_on:
      - redis
volumes:
  pgdata:
  redisdata:
```

In the above, the ***Volumes*** ensure that database and cache data are not lost if containers restart. The **`depends_on`** property ensures startup order, but for actual readiness (e.g., waiting for the database to accept connections), our app should retry connections rather than assume instant availability.

Building and Running Stack

Once everything is in place, we can bring up the entire environment with a single command:

```
docker compose up --build
```

The Compose will build images as needed, create networks, mount volumes, and start all services. As logs stream to the console, we can visit our application at **`http://localhost:8000/`**, inspect the database with any Postgres client, check Redis keys, and monitor background tasks with Flower at **`http://localhost:5555/`**.

While this Compose stack is perfect for development, it also gives us a foundation for real deployments. We can set different values for volumes, secrets, and resources in **`.env`** or override files. For production, we remove **`--reload`**, enforce strong passwords, and use a process manager or orchestration layer (like Kubernetes) as our needs grow.

Log Aggregation

When we run our apps at scale, the plain console logs or even simple log files no longer suffice. We need a unified, searchable, and real-time view of everything that happens across every container and node. This is where the ***ELK stack***—Elasticsearch, Logstash, and Kibana—shines.

The ELK stack gives us three powerful capabilities:

- ***Centralized storage and search*** (Elasticsearch), able to index, filter, and analyze structured and unstructured logs at any scale.
- ***Log shipping and transformation*** (Filebeat and Logstash), collecting logs from every host and container, and forwarding them in a structured, fault-tolerant way.
- ***Rich visualization and alerting*** (Kibana), letting us build dashboards, slice and dice logs by time, error type, or user, and receive immediate alerts if something goes wrong.

With this stack, we turn raw log files into actionable insights, enabling everything from debugging to security monitoring, SLA tracking, and user experience analytics.

Preparing JSON-Formatted Logs

To get the most value from log aggregation, we want our app to emit logs in structured JSON format—making them easy for Filebeat and Elasticsearch to parse, filter, and visualize. Most Python logging libraries support this out of the box. If we use **`structlog`**, **`loguru`**, or the standard library with a JSON formatter, we can configure all app and worker logs to follow the same format.

Following is an example using Python's built-in logging and **`python-json-logger`**:

```
pip install python-json-logger
import logging
from pythonjsonlogger import jsonlogger
logger = logging.getLogger("myapp")
handler = logging.StreamHandler()
formatter = jsonlogger.JsonFormatter()
handler.setFormatter(formatter)
logger.addHandler(handler)
logger.setLevel(logging.INFO)
```

After this, every log entry now appears as a JSON object, ready for shipping to Elasticsearch. The Following is a sample log output:

```
{"levelname": "INFO", "message": "Request handled",
"timestamp": "2024-07-05T12:00:00", "request_id": "abc123",
"status_code": 200}
```

Shipping Logs to Elasticsearch

The ***Filebeat*** is a lightweight log shipper designed for forwarding and centralizing log data. It is perfectly suited for shipping logs from Docker containers or host machines straight to Elasticsearch (or via Logstash if needed). Now, in local development, the Filebeat can be run as a container or installed on the host. And in a Docker Compose stack, we add a Filebeat service that tails our log files.

Following is the example of the docker-compose.yml:

```
 filebeat:
    image: docker.elastic.co/beats/filebeat:8.13.0
    user: root
    volumes:
      - ./filebeat.yml:/usr/share/filebeat/filebeat.yml:ro
      - ./logs:/app/logs:ro
      -
/var/lib/docker/containers:/var/lib/docker/containers:ro
      - /var/run/docker.sock:/var/run/docker.sock
    environment:
      - ELASTICSEARCH_HOST=elasticsearch:9200
    depends_on:
      - elasticsearch
    restart: unless-stopped
```

Given below is the Filebeat configuration i.e. filebeat.yml:

```
filebeat.inputs:
  - type: log
    enabled: true
    paths:
      - /app/logs/*.json
    json.keys_under_root: true
    json.add_error_key: true
output.elasticsearch:
  hosts: ["${ELASTICSEARCH_HOST:elasticsearch:9200}"]
  username: "elastic"
  password: "changeme"    # Use secrets for real deployments
  indices:
    - index: "myapp-logs-%{+yyyy.MM.dd}"
setup.kibana:
```

```
  host: "kibana:5601"
```

In the above,

- We direct Filebeat to pick up all **.json** logs from the mapped directory.
- The **json.keys_under_root** option flattens each JSON object, making all fields searchable in Elasticsearch.
- We configure the Elasticsearch host and index naming pattern for daily rotation.
- And, the Kibana setup is also included for index pattern preconfiguration.

When containers emit logs to **logs/**, Filebeat picks them up and forwards them in real time.

Full Logging Stack Preview

Now that we have Elasticsearch and Kibana in our Compose file, we can add the following services or use the official ELK stack Docker Compose as a reference:

```
 elasticsearch:
    image:
docker.elastic.co/elasticsearch/elasticsearch:8.13.0
    environment:
      - discovery.type=single-node
      - ES_JAVA_OPTS=-Xms1g -Xmx1g
      - ELASTIC_PASSWORD=changeme
    ports:
      - "9200:9200"
    volumes:
      - esdata:/usr/share/elasticsearch/data
  kibana:
    image: docker.elastic.co/kibana/kibana:8.13.0
    environment:
      - ELASTICSEARCH_HOSTS=http://elasticsearch:9200
      - ELASTICSEARCH_USERNAME=elastic
      - ELASTICSEARCH_PASSWORD=changeme
    ports:
      - "5601:5601"
```

```
    depends_on:
      - elasticsearch
volumes:
  esdata:
```

With this, we now have a full stack where:

- ***Elasticsearch*** stores and indexes all logs.
- ***Kibana*** provides a rich UI for visualization and search.
- ***Filebeat*** continuously ships our JSON logs.

By starting the stack with **`docker compose up`**, it brings all the components online.

Kibana Dashboards for Error Rates/Request Metrics

Once the logs flow into Elasticsearch, the Kibana becomes our main window into system health, errors, and usage. For this, we will build a dashboard together.

Creating Index Patterns

- On first login to Kibana (**`http://localhost:5601`**), navigate to Stack Management → Index Patterns.
- Create a pattern that matches our logs, e.g., **`myapp-logs-*`**.
- Select **`timestamp`** as the time field.

Visualizing Error Rates

- Go to "Discover" and verify that log fields (e.g., **`levelname`**, **`status_code`**, **`message`**) are indexed and searchable.
- Build a bar or line chart showing **`count of logs`** over time, filtered by **`levelname: ERROR`** or **`status_code: >=500`**.
- Add this chart to a new Dashboard named "Application Health".

Monitoring Request Metrics

- Visualize **`request_id`** counts or **`status_code`** breakdowns to spot surges or anomalies.
- Create tables or pie charts grouping by endpoint, error type, or user.
- Arrange all widgets, save the dashboard, and set auto-refresh for live monitoring.

Setting up Alerting Rules

To stay ahead of operational issues, we can set up alerts directly in Kibana:

- Navigate to "Stack Management" → "Rules and Connectors".

- Create a new rule, using the "Elasticsearch Query" rule type.

Next, we then define a query such as:

```
levelname: "ERROR" AND @timestamp >= "now-5m"
```

This sets the threshold (e.g., more than 10 errors in 5 minutes). We can configure the action, like send an email, Slack message, or webhook notification. With these rules, the team receives instant alerts on spikes in errors, slow requests, or even unusual user behavior, before the users notice issues.

Once live, this ELK-powered pipeline provides a real-time window into every service and container:

- ***Immediate visibility*** for debugging, post-mortems, and compliance.
- ***Full-text search*** to trace requests, correlate logs by **`request_id`**, or find slow queries.
- ***Drill-down and filtering*** by service, host, or custom application fields.
- ***Long-term retention*** for trend analysis, audits, or performance tuning.

If logs aren't appearing, then we need to check the following:

- The Filebeat container logs for path or permissions issues.
- The Elasticsearch health and disk usage.
- And, the Docker volume mounts for correct paths.

This log aggregation workflow has transformed raw log files into a structured, searchable, alert-driven observability platform. Now, every service is transparent, every error is traceable, and every metric is just a dashboard or alert away. These improvements empower our operations team to scale confidently and respond swiftly to anything production throws our way.

Kubernetes Manifests

The outgrowing of a handful of containers on a single host results in the impossibility of orchestrating, scaling, and managing them by hand. This is where Kubernetes, the industry-standard container orchestrator, steps in, letting us automate the deployment, scaling, networking, and self-healing of services across clusters of nodes. At the heart of Kubernetes operations lies the manifest, which is a plain-text YAML file that describes what we want Kubernetes to run and how it should behave.

A manifest is our contract with the cluster. We define everything from how code runs to how it's accessed, configured, and stores sensitive credentials by declaring Deployments, Services, Ingresses, ConfigMaps, and Secrets. The power of Kubernetes comes from treating these YAML files as the "source of truth." Every infrastructure change is a matter of editing and applying a manifest. This is true whether the change is rolling out a new version, scaling up, rotating a password, or adjusting network access. This practice leads to safer, more repeatable, and more auditable operations.

Writing Kubernetes Deployment Manifest

A ***Deployment*** describes how to run and manage a set of identical Pods—our application containers—in the cluster. We shall specify the container image, resource limits, environment variables, and the number of replicas for high availability.

So here, we will write a deployment manifest:

```
# deployment.yaml
apiVersion: apps/v1
kind: Deployment
metadata:
  name: myapp
  labels:
    app: myapp
spec:
  replicas: 3
  selector:
    matchLabels:
      app: myapp
  template:
    metadata:
      labels:
        app: myapp
    spec:
      containers:
        - name: myapp
          image: myregistry/myapp:1.0.0
          ports:
            - containerPort: 8000
          env:
```

```
            - name: DATABASE_URL
              valueFrom:
                secretKeyRef:
                  name: myapp-secret
                  key: database-url
          resources:
            requests:
              cpu: "250m"
              memory: "512Mi"
            limits:
              cpu: "500m"
              memory: "1Gi"
```

With this, following is what we've established:

- We want three replicas of our app, each exposing port 8000.
- Pods are labeled for easy selection and traffic routing.
- An environment variable (**`DATABASE_URL`**) is pulled from a Secret (see below).
- Resource requests and limits help the scheduler fit pods efficiently on nodes.

Defining Kubernetes Service Manifest

A ***Service*** exposes one or more Pods to other parts of the cluster (and, optionally, to the outside world), providing stable networking despite pods being ephemeral and moving across nodes.

Following is a simple ClusterIP service (internal traffic only):

```
# service.yaml
apiVersion: v1
kind: Service
metadata:
  name: myapp-service
spec:
  selector:
    app: myapp
```

```
  ports:
    - protocol: TCP
      port: 80
      targetPort: 8000
```

In the above, the traffic sent to port 80 of the Service is forwarded to port 8000 in each app pod. The selector ties this Service to pods labeled **`app: myapp`**. For external access, you might use **`type: LoadBalancer`** (cloud) or expose it through Ingress (next step).

Defining Ingress Resource for HTTP Routing

The ***Ingress*** provides advanced HTTP(S) routing to our services, thereby terminating TLS, routing domains, and managing URL paths.

See the below one which is a simple Ingress manifest:

```
# ingress.yaml
apiVersion: networking.k8s.io/v1
kind: Ingress
metadata:
  name: myapp-ingress
  annotations:
    nginx.ingress.kubernetes.io/rewrite-target: /
spec:
  rules:
    - host: myapp.local
      http:
        paths:
          - path: /
            pathType: Prefix
            backend:
              service:
                name: myapp-service
                port:
```

```
                number: 80
```

In the above, all the requests to **`myapp.local/`** route to our Service's port 80. And in production, you can add a TLS section and real domain names.

Using ConfigMap and Secret for Configuration

The kubernetes encourages storing non-sensitive config separately in ***ConfigMaps***, and secrets in ***Secrets***, both as key-value pairs.

Following is the ***ConfigMap*** example:

```
# configmap.yaml
apiVersion: v1
kind: ConfigMap
metadata:
  name: myapp-config
data:
  LOG_LEVEL: "info"
  CACHE_HOST: "redis.default.svc.cluster.local"
```

Then you can reference it in a deployment like the below:

```
envFrom:
  - configMapRef:
      name: myapp-config
```

The given below is a ***Secret*** example, like for sensitive settings, or like DB URLs:

```
# secret.yaml
apiVersion: v1
kind: Secret
metadata:
  name: myapp-secret
type: Opaque
data:
```

```
  database-url:
bXlwZGI6cGFzc3dvcmRAMTI3LjAuMC4xOjU0MzIvbXlkYg==
```

In the above, the values must be base64-encoded (you can use **`echo -n "value" | base64`** to encode). The consuming of the secret in the Deployment is shown above in the env section.

Applying and Managing Manifests

Once manifests are written, we use **`kubectl`** to interact with the cluster. Now, to create or update the resources:

```
kubectl apply -f deployment.yaml
kubectl apply -f service.yaml
kubectl apply -f ingress.yaml
kubectl apply -f configmap.yaml
kubectl apply -f secret.yaml
```

And, if you want to view the resource status:

```
kubectl get deployments
kubectl get pods
kubectl get services
kubectl get ingress
kubectl get configmap
kubectl get secret
```

And, if you wish to inspect the details:

```
kubectl describe deployment myapp
kubectl describe pod myapp-xxxxxxx
```

Performing Rolling Updates

The Kubernetes deployments automatically provide ***rolling updates***, so we can roll out new versions of our app with zero downtime. Let me take you through this tiny process:

- At first, edit the deployment manifest to point to a new image tag (**`myregistry/myapp:1.0.1`**). And then apply the manifest again:

```
kubectl apply -f deployment.yaml
```

- Next, watch the rollout status:

```
kubectl rollout status deployment/myapp
```

After this, the Kubernetes will start new pods, wait until they are healthy, then gradually terminate the old pods. If anything fails (such as readiness or liveness probes), the update halts and can be rolled back.

So now, if you want to see all rollout history:

```
kubectl rollout history deployment/myapp
```

If something goes wrong and you want to revert:

```
kubectl rollout undo deployment/myapp
```

Managing Rollouts and Scaling

By default, the Kubernetes updates a few pods at a time (maxSurge, maxUnavailable). For very sensitive services, you can tune these options. So, to scale the Deployment manually:

```
kubectl scale deployment myapp --replicas=5
```

And, to trigger a restart (for config change or troubleshooting):

```
kubectl rollout restart deployment/myapp
```

Organizing and Versioning Manifests

As our stack grows, we group related manifests into folders:

```
k8s/
  deployment.yaml
  service.yaml
  ingress.yaml
  configmap.yaml
  secret.yaml
```

Many teams store manifests in Git, applying changes through pull requests and CI/CD pipelines, making infrastructure truly version-controlled, repeatable, and auditable.

Overall, when all manifests are applied, we can access our app through the ingress domain, observe live traffic in the cluster, and use built-in Kubernetes dashboards for further monitoring. The logs from pods are instantly accessible, and every scaling or deployment change is a matter of editing a YAML file and re-applying.

Summary

In the end, we created the base for modern deployment and great performance in Python web applications. First, we learned how to use Docker Compose to orchestrate multi-service environments. Then, we configured our Python app alongside supporting containers for databases, caches, and background processing. We crafted multi-stage Dockerfiles to ensure our deployments were lean and secure. Next, we moved into log aggregation. We set up the ELK stack and learned to forward structured JSON logs from our services using Filebeat.

Next, we then created Kibana dashboards to track errors and request patterns and implemented alerting rules to notify us instantly about critical events. As we started to use orchestration at scale, we looked at Kubernetes manifests. We used YAML to describe each service and resource. This included Deployments and Services, Ingress, ConfigMaps, and Secrets. We practiced rolling updates and managed rollout strategies. We also observed how **`kubectl`** commands allowed us to scale, update, and troubleshoot our entire stack. Through these operational skills, we transitioned from manual configuration to infrastructure as code, paving the way for a resilient, observable, and scalable platform.

CHAPTER 8: SECURITY & COMPLIANCE

Overview

This chapter will teach you to build and enforce the multi-layered security and compliance practices that modern applications require. First, you will learn how APIs are vulnerable to cross-site attacks. Then, you will implement robust CSRF and CORS configurations to protect endpoints from unauthorized or malicious requests. You will be walked through writing and managing Content Security Policy headers, and then you will be taught how strict directives are to be authored and their impact on real-world traffic validated.

You will learn to encrypt sensitive fields using AES-GCM, manage encryption keys securely through environment variables, and set up seamless key rotation to maintain data confidentiality. You will enforce transport-level encryption with TLS for every connection to ensure that sensitive data is never exposed in transit. Finally, you will design append-only, timestamped audit logging systems that capture critical events and actions. This will equip the app with traceability and a durable record for compliance and incident response.

CSRF & CORS Configuration

API Threat Landscape

When we expose our APIs to browsers or third-party clients, we face a class of vulnerabilities known as cross-site attacks. Two of the most prevalent are ***Cross-Site Request Forgery (CSRF)*** and ***Cross-Origin Resource Sharing (CORS) exploitation***. Each targets different pieces of the browser's trust model but can be devastating if left unchecked. The ***CSRF*** tricks a user's browser into sending a request to our API—often while the user is authenticated—by embedding a malicious link or form in another site. If our API accepts the request, the attacker can make unwanted changes on behalf of the victim, such as transferring funds, changing passwords, or modifying data, all without the user's knowledge. The key risk is that browsers automatically attach cookies or credentials for sites where the user is already logged in. The ***CORS*** defines which origins (domains) are permitted to make requests to our API from the browser. If our CORS policy is too permissive, malicious sites can interact with our endpoints, sometimes exfiltrating sensitive information or bypassing security controls intended for trusted origins. Modern browsers enforce these rules with preflight requests and strict header checks, but the server's configuration is the final gatekeeper.

FastAPI Middleware for CSRF Protection

The CSRF protection centers around one concept: requiring a secret token on all state-changing (unsafe) requests. Only trusted clients (typically our own frontend) should know and provide this token, which is validated by the server. This prevents attackers from forging requests, even if the user's browser automatically includes credentials.

While FastAPI does not include built-in CSRF middleware, several well-maintained libraries exist for this purpose. One practical approach is to use *fastapi-csrf-protect* or implement a custom solution using signed tokens and dependency injection. In the below, we will use **`fastapi-csrf-protect`** for clarity and maintainability.

So here, at first, we will install the package:

```
pip install fastapi-csrf-protect
```

Next, we will add CSRF middleware to our FastAPI project:

```
from fastapi import FastAPI, Request, Depends, HTTPException
from fastapi.responses import JSONResponse
from fastapi_csrf_protect import CsrfProtect
from fastapi_csrf_protect.exceptions import CsrfProtectError
from pydantic import BaseModel
class CsrfSettings(BaseModel):
    secret_key: str = "your-very-secret-key"  # Use a secure
key in production
app = FastAPI()
@CsrfProtect.load_config
def get_csrf_config():
    return CsrfSettings()
@app.exception_handler(CsrfProtectError)
def csrf_exception_handler(request: Request, exc:
CsrfProtectError):
    return JSONResponse(
        status_code=exc.status_code,
        content={"detail": exc.message}
    )
```

This initializes CSRF protection with a secret key (which should be kept private and rotated in production). We can also set up an exception handler to catch and respond to CSRF violations in a consistent manner.

While you do, you must understand how the token exchange works?

For all state-changing requests (POST, PUT, PATCH, DELETE), the client must provide a valid CSRF token. The server generates this token and shares it with the client (often as a cookie or response header). On each protected request, the client reads the token and submits it as a header (e.g., **X-CSRF-Token**). The server validates the token against the session or signed data.

So here, we will implement this pattern in our app.

and Validating CSRF Tokens

Let us assume that we want to protect all POST requests to **/account/update**:

```
from fastapi import Form
@app.get("/csrf-token")
def get_csrf(csrf_protect: CsrfProtect = Depends()):
    # This endpoint issues a fresh CSRF token
    csrf_token = csrf_protect.generate_csrf()
    return {"csrf_token": csrf_token}
@app.post("/account/update")
def update_account(
    csrf_protect: CsrfProtect = Depends(),
    username: str = Form(...),
    email: str = Form(...),
    csrf_token: str = Form(...)
):
    # Validate CSRF token on any state-changing request
    csrf_protect.validate_csrf(csrf_token)
    # Proceed with account update logic
    return {"msg": "Account updated"}
```

In the above,

- The client (e.g., our JavaScript SPA) first fetches **/csrf-token** to get a valid token, then submits it with any protected form.
- On every update, the server checks the token before proceeding.
- For AJAX, the CSRF token is typically sent as a header; for HTML forms, it may be a hidden field.

Configuring CORS Origins and Allowed Methods

The CORS policies define exactly which web origins are allowed to communicate with our API and under what conditions. FastAPI provides a ready-to-use middleware for fine-grained CORS control.

In the following, we will learn to configure the strict CORS:

```
from fastapi.middleware.cors import CORSMiddleware
origins = [
    "https://trusted-frontend.com",
    "https://admin-panel.company.com"
]
app.add_middleware(
    CORSMiddleware,
    allow_origins=origins,                    # Only these
origins can use the API
    allow_credentials=True,                   # Allow cookies or
HTTP auth
    allow_methods=["GET", "POST", "PUT", "DELETE", "OPTIONS"],
# Permitted HTTP methods
    allow_headers=["Authorization", "Content-Type", "X-CSRF-
Token"],  # Permitted headers
)
```

In this configuration,

- we prevent arbitrary sites from accessing our API.
- The credentials are enabled only when truly required.
- The allowed methods and headers are narrowed to exactly what our frontend needs.

Testing Preflight Requests

The majority of modern browsers enforce CORS policies by sending a ***preflight*** OPTIONS request before most cross-origin POST, PUT, or DELETE requests. Essentially, the browser asks the server, "Am I allowed to send this request with these headers/methods from this origin?"

Luckily, the FastAPI's CORS Middleware handles these preflight checks automatically. Below, we will simulate how this looks, wherein the browser issues an OPTIONS request to

/account/update, with following headers:

```
Origin: https://trusted-frontend.com
Access-Control-Request-Method: POST
Access-Control-Request-Headers: X-CSRF-Token, Content-Type
```

The FastAPI then replies with:

```
Access-Control-Allow-Origin: https://trusted-frontend.com
Access-Control-Allow-Methods: GET, POST, PUT, DELETE, OPTIONS
Access-Control-Allow-Headers: Authorization, Content-Type, X-
CSRF-Token
```

If the origin or headers do not match the allowed list, the browser blocks the request before it even reaches our backend logic.

Testing With HTTP Clients

Here, we can use **curl** or browser developer tools to simulate and verify preflight scenarios:

```
curl -X OPTIONS http://localhost:8000/account/update \
  -H "Origin: https://trusted-frontend.com" \
  -H "Access-Control-Request-Method: POST" \
  -H "Access-Control-Request-Headers: X-CSRF-Token,Content-
Type" \
  -i
```

The response should include the correct **Access-Control-Allow-*** headers only for trusted origins.

Testing State-Changing Requests

For a POST request from the frontend:

- The request must include both the CSRF token (header or form field) and come from an allowed CORS origin.
- Any failure in token validation or CORS policy leads to a blocked or rejected request.

In production, CSRF and CORS are typically paired with authentication middleware, rate limiting, and logging for a defense-in-depth posture. The FastAPI's middleware and dependency patterns make these protections straightforward and adaptable, and by testing preflight and real-world requests, we ensure every state-changing API is guarded by layers of automated policy.

Content Security Policy Headers

With the explosion of JavaScript-powered frontends, browser plugins, and third-party integrations, web apps are more powerful—but also more vulnerable—than ever before. Malicious actors can exploit every window the browser provides, from reflected XSS attacks and script injection to style manipulation and data exfiltration. Even a minor vulnerability can compromise the entire platform.

The ***Content Security Policy (CSP)*** headers provide a robust, flexible, and modern way to enforce which sources of content like, scripts, styles, images, fonts, and more, are trusted on our pages. When used well, CSPs can neutralize entire classes of browser-based attacks, especially Cross-Site Scripting (XSS), by refusing to execute code that doesn't come from explicitly permitted origins.

A CSP header works by instructing the browser: "Only trust content from these sources. Block and report everything else." This turns the browser itself into an enforcement agent, stopping malicious behavior before it even reaches our code.

Designing Strict CSP Directives

The CSP policies are defined as a series of directives. Each directive controls which sources are allowed for a particular content type. The strictest (and safest) approach is to permit only what's truly required.

Following are the common directives which include:

- ***default-src***: fallback for all content types.
- ***script-src***: allowed JavaScript sources.
- ***style-src***: allowed CSS sources.
- ***img-src***: allowed image sources.
- ***font-src***: allowed font sources.
- ***connect-src***: allowed endpoints for XHR, fetch, or WebSockets.

Let us see how a strict, default-deny policy might look like this:

```
Content-Security-Policy:
  default-src 'none';
  script-src 'self';
  style-src 'self';
  img-src 'self' data:;
  font-src 'self';
```

```
    connect-src 'self' api.trusted.com;
    object-src 'none';
    frame-ancestors 'none';
```

All of these settings mean that:

- Only scripts, styles, images, fonts, and network connections from the same origin (**'self'**) are allowed.
- Inline scripts and styles are blocked unless explicitly allowed (not recommended).
- Images can be loaded from the same origin or as data URIs.
- No plugins, frames, or objects are permitted.

We dramatically reduce our attack surface by starting from the strictest base and only adding exceptions as required, such as for third-party analytics and content delivery networks (CDNs).

Injecting CSP Headers

The FastAPI is built on Starlette, which makes it straightforward to add custom middleware for HTTP headers, including CSP. We will walk through adding strict CSP headers to every response. And here, we'll author our policy as a constant string, then build and register custom middleware.

```
from fastapi import FastAPI, Request, Response
from starlette.middleware.base import BaseHTTPMiddleware
CSP_POLICY = (
    "default-src 'none'; "
    "script-src 'self'; "
    "style-src 'self'; "
    "img-src 'self' data:; "
    "font-src 'self'; "
    "connect-src 'self' https://api.trusted.com; "
    "object-src 'none'; "
    "frame-ancestors 'none';"
)
class ContentSecurityPolicyMiddleware(BaseHTTPMiddleware):
    async def dispatch(self, request: Request, call_next):
        response: Response = await call_next(request)
```

```
        response.headers['Content-Security-Policy'] =
CSP_POLICY
        return response
app = FastAPI()
app.add_middleware(ContentSecurityPolicyMiddleware)
```

With this middleware registered, every outgoing HTTP response will carry the CSP header. The browser will instantly enforce these rules on every page load. For most APIs and admin panels, a single strict policy applies everywhere. If you serve both API and HTML routes from the same app, you can conditionally inject different CSPs depending on the request path.

Inline Script and Style Allowances

The CSP is most visible when it blocks something the page tries to load. The browsers will refuse to run or render content that violates the policy, and surface clear errors in their developer consoles.

Testing Inline Script Blocking

By default, our policy (**`script-src 'self'`**) prohibits all inline scripts (including **`<script>alert("hi")</script>`** and even some JavaScript event attributes in HTML).

If a page includes:

```
<script>
  console.log('This will be blocked');
</script>
```

The browser console logs a CSP error, and the script does not execute.

Allowing Inline Scripts

To allow inline scripts, we could add **`'unsafe-inline'`** to the policy:

```
CSP_POLICY = (
    "default-src 'none'; "
    "script-src 'self' 'unsafe-inline'; "
    # ...
)
```

However, this is discouraged except for legacy code or unavoidable cases, as it re-opens XSS risks.

Testing Inline Style Blocking

Similarly, only external or **`<style>`** blocks sourced from the same origin are allowed by default. Inline **`style=""`** attributes or **`<style>`** tags with inline CSS may be blocked.

Again, **`'unsafe-inline'`** can be added to the **`style-src`** for legacy support, but it's safer to avoid.

Testing Remote Scripts/Styles

If you load assets from CDNs or trusted partners, add their origins to the respective directives, for example:

```
script-src 'self' https://cdn.jsdelivr.net;
style-src 'self' https://fonts.googleapis.com;
```

Every additional source should be carefully reviewed and justified.

Over time, we monitor browser console logs, scan CSP reports, and update our policy to accommodate new features or integrations, always prioritizing a default-deny, explicit-allow strategy.

Data Encryption

The cryptography world has evolved over decades, but today, ***AES-GCM*** (Advanced Encryption Standard in Galois/Counter Mode) stands as the preferred algorithm for most modern applications. It is both secure and performant, widely audited, and natively supported by almost every cloud platform and language runtime. AES-GCM offers strong authenticated encryption, which means it not only protects confidentiality but also guarantees that no tampering has occurred, if any part of the data changes, decryption fails. This all-in-one approach is why regulatory standards (such as HIPAA, PCI DSS, and GDPR) cite AES-GCM as an acceptable method for storing and exchanging sensitive data.

With AES-GCM, encryption and authentication are handled in a single pass, making it suitable for high-traffic APIs and background jobs alike. It also introduces the concept of a nonce (number used once) for every operation, reducing the risk of certain attack classes.

Implementing AES-GCM Encryption

We will walk through encrypting and decrypting fields in our FastAPI app using the **`cryptography`** library, a well-maintained and widely trusted Python package.

At first, we install the required package:

```
pip install cryptography
```

We will then create a utility module, **crypto_utils.py**, for reusable, testable encryption logic:

```
import os
from cryptography.hazmat.primitives.ciphers.aead import AESGCM
def get_aesgcm_key() -> bytes:
    # Get a 256-bit key from an environment variable
    key = os.environ.get("AES_GCM_KEY")
    if not key:
        raise ValueError("Missing AES_GCM_KEY in environment")
    return bytes.fromhex(key)
def encrypt_field(plaintext: str) -> dict:
    aesgcm = AESGCM(get_aesgcm_key())
    nonce = os.urandom(12)  # GCM standard nonce size
    ct = aesgcm.encrypt(nonce, plaintext.encode(), None)
    return {
        "nonce": nonce.hex(),
        "ciphertext": ct.hex()
    }
def decrypt_field(nonce_hex: str, ct_hex: str) -> str:
    aesgcm = AESGCM(get_aesgcm_key())
    nonce = bytes.fromhex(nonce_hex)
    ct = bytes.fromhex(ct_hex)
    plaintext = aesgcm.decrypt(nonce, ct, None)
    return plaintext.decode()
```

By doing this,

- Each field is encrypted using AES-GCM with a 256-bit key.
- A new, random 12-byte nonce is generated per encryption (never reused).

- The output is a pair of hex-encoded values: **nonce** and **ciphertext**.
- For decryption, we supply both the stored nonce and ciphertext.

When saving sensitive fields (like **ssn**, **api_secret**, or **payment_token**), we store both the ciphertext and its nonce in separate columns or as a JSON field. This makes decryption on read straightforward and keeps the implementation stateless.

Applying Field-Level Encryption

We will walk through a state-changing endpoint that encrypts data before storing it:

```
from fastapi import APIRouter, HTTPException
from .crypto_utils import encrypt_field, decrypt_field
router = APIRouter()
@router.post("/secrets/store")
async def store_secret(user_id: str, secret_value: str):
    encrypted = encrypt_field(secret_value)
    # Store encrypted["nonce"] and encrypted["ciphertext"] in
DB, associated with user_id
    # ... (ORM logic here)
    return {"msg": "Secret stored securely."}
@router.get("/secrets/{user_id}")
async def get_secret(user_id: str):
    # Retrieve nonce and ciphertext for user_id from DB
    # ... (ORM logic here)
    try:
        plaintext = decrypt_field(stored_nonce, stored_ct)
    except Exception:
        raise HTTPException(status_code=400,
detail="Decryption failed")
    return {"secret": plaintext}
```

With this workflow, the secrets are never exposed at rest, and can only be decrypted by application logic that holds the right key.

Managing Encryption Keys

The key management is where most encryption schemes fail in real-world deployments. Hard-coding keys, storing them in source control, or neglecting to rotate them are common mistakes that can undo even the strongest cryptography.

Let us take an example of setting the key. At first, we will generate a random 256-bit key:

```
python -c "import os; print(os.urandom(32).hex())"
```

We then set in our environment or **`.env`** file:

```
AES_GCM_KEY=... (hex string here) ...
```

For key rotation, we then deploy a new key as an additional environment variable (e.g., **`AES_GCM_KEY_NEW`**). On every write, we encrypt with the new key. On read, we try the new key first; if decryption fails, fall back to the old key. And, once all old data is migrated (re-encrypted with the new key), we then retire the old key.

Enforcing TLS for All Network Communication

No matter how robust our field-level encryption, it is only as secure as the channel it travels through. Unencrypted HTTP exposes all traffic—including authentication tokens, user data, and even the encrypted blobs themselves—to interception and manipulation.

The ***TLS (Transport Layer Security)*** is non-negotiable for all production traffic, both external and internal (service-to-service). Although FastAPI itself does not directly serve TLS (since it's designed to run behind a reverse proxy), you can enforce HTTPS by checking the request scheme:

```
from fastapi import Request
from fastapi.responses import RedirectResponse
@app.middleware("http")
async def https_redirect_middleware(request: Request,
call_next):
    if request.url.scheme != "https":
        url = request.url.replace(scheme="https")
        return RedirectResponse(str(url))
    return await call_next(request)
```

In production, most TLS enforcement should happen at the proxy or load balancer layer, not in application code.

By weaving together robust field-level AES-GCM encryption, disciplined key management, and unwavering enforcement of TLS for all traffic, our application delivers true defense in depth. These patterns are both a technical and compliance baseline—protecting user data even if databases or backups are compromised, and keeping attackers out at every layer of the stack.

Audit Logging

The audit logs provide an indelible record of what happened, who did it, and when. The audit trails help you to assess the incidents, support compliance audits, and even resolve user disputes. They also act as a deterrent: when users know their actions are logged, risky or malicious activity becomes less likely.

Unlike standard application logs, the audit logs must be:

- ***Append-only***—entries are never updated or deleted.
- ***Timestamped***—every record includes an immutable time of action.
- ***Attributable***—each event is tied to a specific user or system identity.
- ***Structured***—easy to query, filter, and export.

We will now implement an audit logging strategy that sits alongside our main application data, capturing sensitive operations like logins, role changes, data exports, deletions, and permission escalations.

Designing Audit Log Table

A good audit table is simple but powerful. Given below is a typical structure using SQLAlchemy ORM as an example:

```
from sqlalchemy import Column, String, DateTime, JSON
from sqlalchemy.dialects.postgresql import UUID
from sqlalchemy.ext.declarative import declarative_base
import uuid
from datetime import datetime
Base = declarative_base()
class AuditLog(Base):
    __tablename__ = "audit_logs"
    id = Column(UUID(as_uuid=True), primary_key=True,
default=uuid.uuid4)
    user_id = Column(String, nullable=False)
```

```
    action = Column(String, nullable=False)
    timestamp = Column(DateTime, default=datetime.utcnow,
nullable=False)
    resource = Column(String, nullable=True)
    metadata = Column(JSON, nullable=True)  # For extra
details (IP, payload, etc)
```

This above table should never be modified in place; no **UPDATE** or **DELETE** operations are permitted on audit logs.

Capturing Audit Events in Application

Now every time a critical operation occurs, an audit log entry is created and written to the database. This is best handled in a dedicated utility function or decorator, to reduce the risk of developer oversight.

Following is a simple audit logging utility:

```
from sqlalchemy.orm import Session
def log_audit_event(
    db: Session,
    user_id: str,
    action: str,
    resource: str = None,
    metadata: dict = None
):
    entry = AuditLog(
        user_id=user_id,
        action=action,
        resource=resource,
        metadata=metadata or {}
    )
    db.add(entry)
    db.commit()
```

Following is a quick examples of its use in a FastAPI endpoint:

```
from fastapi import Depends, HTTPException, Request
from sqlalchemy.orm import Session
@app.post("/users/{user_id}/promote")
def promote_user(
    user_id: str,
    db: Session = Depends(get_db),
    current_user: str = Depends(get_current_user)
):
    # ... perform promotion logic ...
    log_audit_event(
        db=db,
        user_id=current_user,
        action="promote_user",
        resource=user_id,
        metadata={"role": "admin", "ip":
str(Request.client.host)}
    )
    return {"msg": "User promoted"}
```

Here, every promotion event is recorded, including who did it, who was affected, when, and extra context. The use of similar calls is required for logins, password changes, data exports, and deletions.

Querying and Monitoring Audit Logs

The audit logs are only useful if you can figure out what they mean. We should expose filtered, paginated queries for admin dashboards. You can set up alerts for sensitive actions, like sudden bursts of deletions, repeated failed logins, or privilege escalations.

You can integrate it with our existing ELK or SIEM systems for centralized monitoring. Following is an example showing how to fetch all admin role changes in the last 24 hours:

```
from datetime import datetime, timedelta
recent_admin_changes = db.query(AuditLog).filter(
```

```
    AuditLog.action == "promote_user",
    AuditLog.timestamp >= datetime.utcnow() - 
timedelta(days=1)
).all()
```

After implementation, every key action leaves a durable, searchable record. Incidents can be reconstructed; access can be proven; compliance audits are simplified. Users, administrators, and even auditors can have confidence that the system can reveal exactly what happened and when—without gaps or ambiguity.

Summary

So, we put together a solid security and compliance plan for our app. We started by understanding the risks of cross-site attacks, like CSRF and CORS. Then, we put in place some practical protections using FastAPI middleware. This meant enforcing strict CSRF token validation and precise CORS rules for all state-changing API requests. We crafted and injected robust Content Security Policy headers, learning to author strict CSP directives and to observe their effect on inline scripts and styles.

We've got a pretty solid workflow for keeping sensitive data protected. It includes things like AES-GCM encryption, field-level utilities, environment-based key management, and routine key rotation strategies. We made sure all communications were over TLS to further reduce attack surfaces. The chapter ended with audit logging, where we recorded important user actions in records that can't be changed and have a timestamp, creating a tamper-resistant trail that's essential for following regulations and making sure everything is clear and open.

CHAPTER 9: TESTING & CI/CD

Overview

This chapter's going to teach you how to build a complete, modern testing and continuous integration pipeline that supports both developer productivity and organizational reliability. You'll start by getting a handle on unit testing with Pytest. You'll learn how to isolate business logic, use fixtures for reusable setup, and use mocking to separate tests from external systems. The chapter will then show you how to do integration testing, giving you an idea of how to run dependent services like Redis in Docker containers and validate realistic, end-to-end API workflows. It'll be your job to construct and customize a GitHub Actions pipeline, automating every step from code linting to Docker image builds and registry pushes, all with security and traceability in mind.

We'll be weaving coverage reporting into our workflow, which will let you see where there are gaps in coverage, generate HTML reports, and make sure we have minimum standards in CI. That way, we can stop untested code from getting into our mainline. When you're done reading this, you'll know how to design and run a CI/CD system that keeps our software safe, easy to maintain, and always ready for delivery.

Unit Testing with Pytest

The point of testing isn't just to make sure everything's good to go—it's also about making sure we can make those bold code changes we're known for. It's a simple fact that when tests are easy to write, fast to run, and rich in feedback, our development velocity accelerates. For most new Python projects, Pytest is the go-to choice. It doesn't need a lot of extra code, it lets you make strong statements, and it works great with the rest of our tools. It's easy to use Pytest to validate every branch, catch regressions, and make sure our business rules stay true as features grow. It's got a bunch of plugins, a flexible fixture model, and tight integration with tools for coverage, mocking, and reporting. Pytest makes it a breeze to go from a few tests to thousands.

Writing Pytest Functions

We begin by testing "pure" functions: those with no side effects or dependencies. Pytest discovers all files named **test_*.py** or ***_test.py**, and finds any function prefixed with **test_**. Each test is just a standard Python function, with regular **assert** statements.

Suppose we have a utility function in **utils/math_utils.py**:

```
def add_numbers(a, b):
    return a + b
def is_even(n):
    return n % 2 == 0
```

To test these, create **tests/test_math_utils.py**:

```
from utils.math_utils import add_numbers, is_even
def test_add_numbers():
    assert add_numbers(2, 3) == 5
    assert add_numbers(-1, 1) == 0
    assert add_numbers(0, 0) == 0
def test_is_even():
    assert is_even(4) is True
    assert is_even(7) is False
```

The running of **pytest** in the project root will discover and execute all tests, reporting every pass and failure with rich, readable output. Pytest captures stack traces and variable values for failed assertions, speeding up diagnosis.

Fixtures for Setup and Teardown

It's rare to find real-world applications that operate in a silo. A lot of functions or classes need a known state. That could be an initialized object, a database connection, a populated temp file, or even a user session. Pytest's fixture system lets us define reusable, parameterizable, and scope-controlled setup logic that can be injected into any test function by name.

Suppose we're testing code that interacts with a database, or needs to clean up after itself. So here, we define a fixture in **tests/conftest.py**:

```
import pytest
import tempfile
import os
@pytest.fixture
def temp_file():
    # Setup: create a temporary file
    fd, path = tempfile.mkstemp()
    os.close(fd)
    yield path
    # Teardown: remove the file after the test
    if os.path.exists(path):
```

```
        os.remove(path)
```

Then we use it in any test:

```
def test_write_and_read(temp_file):
    with open(temp_file, "w") as f:
        f.write("hello world")
    with open(temp_file, "r") as f:
        data = f.read()
    assert data == "hello world"
```

The Pytest guarantees that the fixture is set up before the test runs and torn down afterward—even if an assertion fails. Fixtures can have any scope (**function**, **module**, **session**) and can depend on other fixtures, enabling powerful, layered setups.

Mocking External Dependencies

The true unit tests never cross system boundaries. If a function or method calls out to an API, reads a file, or sends an email, we want to replace ("mock") that dependency with a controlled, predictable stand-in, so our tests are fast, deterministic, and never flaky due to network or service failures.

The Pytest integrates smoothly with Python's standard **unittest.mock** library. The most common pattern uses **patch** to swap out a dependency for the test's duration. Let us say that we have an email utility in **utils/email_utils.py**:

```
def send_email(to, subject, body):
    # Imagine this function actually sends an email
    pass
def notify_user(user, msg):
    subject = "Notification"
    send_email(user.email, subject, msg)
```

Here, we want to test **notify_user** without actually sending an email:

```
from utils.email_utils import notify_user
from unittest.mock import patch, MagicMock
def test_notify_user():
```

```
    user = type("User", (), {"email": "test@example.com"})()
    with patch("utils.email_utils.send_email") as mock_send:
        notify_user(user, "Hello!")
        mock_send.assert_called_once_with("test@example.com",
"Notification", "Hello!")
```

Here,

- **patch** replaces **send_email** with a mock for the scope of the **with** block.
- We assert that it was called with the expected arguments—verifying our business logic, but not relying on real email sending.
- Any other function, method, or object can be mocked—databases, HTTP clients, or external SDKs.

For code that relies on environment variables, time, or random values, **monkeypatch** (a pytest builtin) is also useful:

```
def test_time_dependent_logic(monkeypatch):
    import datetime
    class FakeDateTime:
        @classmethod
        def utcnow(cls):
            return datetime.datetime(2020, 1, 1)
    monkeypatch.setattr("datetime.datetime", FakeDateTime)
    # ...run assertions that rely on this time...
```

For every critical business rule, security check, or complex branch, write a test. Pytest's assert introspection and fixture-driven setup will make it easy to diagnose failures and keep test code clean as production code evolves.

Integration Testing

There are some small pieces of code that we need to test on their own to make sure they're working right. But we also need to make sure that they work well together in the real world. The integration tests bring up real services like databases, caches, and message brokers along with our app, making sure everything works together just like it will in production. This kind of test can find those pesky little bugs that only show up when data goes through a bunch of layers, when you're short on time, or when the data hits different networks. They also let us check the side effects: did the API write to Redis, update the database, and trigger the right notifications, all in one go?

While integration tests are a bit slower than unit tests, they're worth it because they give you peace of mind for every deployment and alert you to any regressions or misconfigurations.

Spinning up Test Containers

We want every integration test run to begin with a known-good environment. Docker Compose makes this repeatable and portable, letting us start (and destroy) real services like Redis in seconds, isolated from the developer's machine and from other tests.

Setting up Docker Compose File for Tests

Suppose we have the following **docker-compose.test.yml** just for integration tests:

```
version: "3.9"
services:
  redis:
    image: redis:7
    ports:
      - "6379:6379"
    healthcheck:
      test: ["CMD", "redis-cli", "ping"]
      interval: 2s
      timeout: 2s
      retries: 5
```

In the above, the **healthcheck** ensures the service is ready before tests begin. The Redis port is exposed locally so our test client can connect.

Tearing Down Services

To do this, simply run the services with:

```
docker compose -f docker-compose.test.yml up -d
```

This command runs Redis in the background for our tests. After tests complete:

```
docker compose -f docker-compose.test.yml down -v
```

The **-v** flag cleans up all volumes, ensuring a fresh state for the next run. You can script this in our CI/CD pipeline or wrap it in a Makefile for convenience.

Running Full API Request Sequences

To truly validate integration, we want to issue real HTTP requests to our FastAPI app, exercising endpoints as a client would. FastAPI ships with a **TestClient** (built on Starlette's test client), which lets us run API calls in memory—or, for a more production-like test, against the app running in Docker, pointed at our real test Redis.

Suppose we have a FastAPI endpoint that sets and retrieves a value from Redis:

```
from fastapi import FastAPI, HTTPException
import redis
app = FastAPI()
r = redis.Redis(host="localhost", port=6379,
decode_responses=True)
@app.post("/cache/set")
def set_value(key: str, value: str):
    r.set(key, value)
    return {"msg": "set"}
@app.get("/cache/get")
def get_value(key: str):
    value = r.get(key)
    if value is None:
        raise HTTPException(status_code=404, detail="Not
found")
    return {"value": value}
```

We then write an integration test with the following script in the **tests/integration/test_cache.py**:

```
import pytest
from fastapi.testclient import TestClient
from app.main import app
client = TestClient(app)
```

```
@pytest.fixture(scope="module", autouse=True)
def setup_redis():
    # Ensure Redis is clean before tests
    import redis
    r = redis.Redis(host="localhost", port=6379)
    r.flushdb()
    yield
    r.flushdb()
def test_set_and_get_value():
    # Set a value
    response = client.post("/cache/set", params={"key": "foo",
"value": "bar"})
    assert response.status_code == 200
    # Retrieve it
    response = client.get("/cache/get", params={"key": "foo"})
    assert response.status_code == 200
    assert response.json()["value"] == "bar"
def test_get_missing_value():
    response = client.get("/cache/get", params={"key":
"missing"})
    assert response.status_code == 404
```

In the above script, the fixture flushes Redis before and after tests, ensuring isolation. Each test runs API calls just as a client would. And, the full request/response flow is validated: data passes through the HTTP layer, app logic, Redis client, and back.

Validating End-to-End Workflows

When we say "real integration tests," we're talking about tests that go beyond a single endpoint. They make sure that when you do a series of actions, you get the right results, transitions in the state, and side effects across services. This could mean chaining API calls, checking the database or cache state, and even making sure logs or notifications are being sent.

For example, testing a multi-step workflow, like suppose our API supports user signup, login, and then storing a value in Redis under their session.

```
def test_signup_login_and_store(client):
    # 1. Signup
    resp = client.post("/auth/signup", json={"username":
"bob", "password": "secret"})
    assert resp.status_code == 201
    # 2. Login
    resp = client.post("/auth/login", data={"username": "bob",
"password": "secret"})
    assert resp.status_code == 200
    token = resp.json()["access_token"]
    headers = {"Authorization": f"Bearer {token}"}
    # 3. Store a value in Redis, authenticated
    resp = client.post("/cache/set", params={"key": "testkey",
"value": "testval"}, headers=headers)
    assert resp.status_code == 200
    # 4. Retrieve it
    resp = client.get("/cache/get", params={"key": "testkey"},
headers=headers)
    assert resp.status_code == 200
    assert resp.json()["value"] == "testval"
```

In the above, each step builds on the previous one, ensuring that authentication, business logic, and cross-service integration all work as intended.

We do this by developing integration tests that use Docker Compose to spin up real services, orchestrate full API request sequences, and validate complete workflows. This closes the gap between code and reality. Our platform gets stronger and more future-proof, so you can deliver things with confidence and consistency.

GitHub Actions Pipeline

The CI is the backbone of reliable, fast-moving software projects. GitHub Actions gives us a native, cloud-hosted solution for running builds, checks, and deployments automatically with every pull request or code push—right where our source lives. Workflows are versioned, visible, and shareable, making them easy to update as requirements grow. By codifying our workflow in

YAML, we document and enforce standards for code quality, correctness, and release hygiene.

Organizing Workflow

The workflows in GitHub Actions live in the **.github/workflows/** directory of our repository. Each workflow is a separate YAML file (e.g., **ci.yml**), and you can have as many as needed for different concerns (e.g., build, release, deploy).

So here, we'll define a single workflow covering:

- Code linting with **flake8**.
- Unit and integration tests with **pytest**.
- Docker image build.
- Docker image push (on main branch or tags).

Defining YAML Workflow

Next, we then create **.github/workflows/ci.yml** in our repo:

```
name: CI/CD Pipeline
on:
  push:
    branches: [ main ]
    tags: [ '*' ]
  pull_request:
    branches: [ main ]
jobs:
  lint:
    runs-on: ubuntu-latest
    steps:
      - name: Checkout code
        uses: actions/checkout@v4
      - name: Set up Python
        uses: actions/setup-python@v5
        with:
          python-version: '3.11'
```

```
      - name: Install dependencies
        run: |
          python -m pip install --upgrade pip
          pip install flake8
      - name: Run flake8 linter
        run: flake8 app/ tests/
  test:
    runs-on: ubuntu-latest
    needs: lint
    services:
      redis:
        image: redis:7
        ports:
          - 6379:6379
    steps:
      - name: Checkout code
        uses: actions/checkout@v4
      - name: Set up Python
        uses: actions/setup-python@v5
        with:
          python-version: '3.11'
      - name: Install dependencies
        run: |
          python -m pip install --upgrade pip
          pip install -r requirements.txt
          pip install pytest pytest-cov
      - name: Run unit and integration tests
        env:
          REDIS_HOST: localhost
```

```
            REDIS_PORT: 6379
          run: pytest --maxfail=2 --disable-warnings --cov=app
tests/
  build-and-push:
    runs-on: ubuntu-latest
    needs: test
    if: github.ref == 'refs/heads/main' ||
startsWith(github.ref, 'refs/tags/')
    steps:
      - name: Checkout code
        uses: actions/checkout@v4
      - name: Set up Docker Buildx
        uses: docker/setup-buildx-action@v3
      - name: Log in to DockerHub
        uses: docker/login-action@v3
        with:
          username: ${{ secrets.DOCKERHUB_USERNAME }}
          password: ${{ secrets.DOCKERHUB_TOKEN }}
      - name: Build Docker image
        run: |
          docker build -t ${{ secrets.DOCKERHUB_USERNAME
}}/myapp:${{ github.sha }} .
      - name: Push Docker image
        run: |
          docker push ${{ secrets.DOCKERHUB_USERNAME
}}/myapp:${{ github.sha }}
```

Building and Pushing Docker Images

The **build-and-push** job only runs on pushes to **main** or on tags (i.e., not on every PR). It first logs in to DockerHub using credentials you store as GitHub secrets (**DOCKERHUB_USERNAME**, **DOCKERHUB_TOKEN**). The Docker image is tagged with the current commit SHA—uniquely identifying each build. The image is then pushed to our Docker registry, making it instantly available for deploys, staging, or further testing. You can adapt the **docker build** and **docker push** commands to support multiple tags (for main, staging, or versioned releases).

Extending Pipeline

If you're working on more advanced workflows, you can use Docker Composer steps to set up environments that integrate multiple services. We've got you covered with actions for Slack, Teams, or email notifications on failures or deployments. After a successful build, images should be automatically deployed to a staging environment or Kubernetes cluster. And use actions/cache to cache dependencies for faster builds. If you need to share build outputs, use the actions/upload-artifact and actions/download-artifact.

See the following example of notifying the Slack upon failure:

```
    - name: Notify Slack on failure
      if: failure()
      uses: 8398a7/action-slack@v3
      with:
        status: ${{ job.status }}
        fields:
repo,message,commit,author,action,eventName,ref,workflow,job,t
ook
      env:
        SLACK_WEBHOOK_URL: ${{ secrets.SLACK_WEBHOOK_URL }}
```

With a full-featured GitHub Actions pipeline, covering lint, test, build, and deploy, we can create a development culture of speed, quality, and confidence. It's all checked, every build is reproducible, and every deploy is traceable, so our software evolves safely and predictably as our ambitions grow.

Coverage Reporting

No matter how thorough your test suite is, there will always be gaps. These gaps could be branches, edge cases, or entire modules that aren't actually exercised by any test. With test coverage, we can see what's being tested and what's not. While 100% coverage doesn't guarantee bug-free code, low or shrinking coverage almost always signals growing risk.

The monitoring, reporting, and enforcing of the minimum coverage helps us to gain:

- Immediate feedback on code quality as features evolve.
- Visibility into neglected modules or hard-to-test branches.
- Confidence that refactors or new features haven't silently eroded safety nets.

With **coverage.py**, we have a mature, flexible, and easy-to-integrate solution for Python test coverage.

Integrating 'coverage.py' with Pytest

In order to integrate, we need to install both **pytest-cov** and **coverage**:

```
pip install pytest-cov coverage
```

The **pytest-cov** integrates coverage measurement seamlessly with pytest, and the **coverage** provides CLI tools for generating detailed reports.

We can also measure coverage simply by adding the **--cov** flag:

```
pytest --cov=app tests/
```

Here, the **--cov=app** tells coverage to monitor the **app/** directory. After running, you'll see a coverage summary right in our terminal: which files were executed and what percent of lines were covered.

Generating Rich HTML Coverage Reports

The terminal summaries are useful, but HTML reports provide visual, line-by-line insight into untested code.

If we want to generate an HTML report, we simply run pytest with coverage, and then outputting results to a file:

```
pytest --cov=app --cov-report=term --cov-report=html tests/
```

In the above, the **--cov-report=term** shows a summary in the console, and the **--cov-report=html** writes a browsable report to the **htmlcov/** directory by default.

We can also customize the reports, such as we can exclude lines with **# pragma: no cover** for intentionally untestable code. We need to simply configure what gets included/excluded in **.coveragerc**:

```
[run]
omit =
    */tests/*
```

```
    */migrations/*
```

This keeps our coverage metric focused on the code that matters.

Enforcing Minimum Coverage Thresholds in CI

The high coverage is only useful if it's maintained. If we enforce the thresholds in CI (such as with GitHub Actions), we prevent untested code from being merged. So if we want to enforce the coverage in Pytest, we simply add the **--cov-fail-under** flag:

```
pytest --cov=app --cov-fail-under=85 tests/
```

This fails the test run if coverage drops below 85%. The CI job fails and code cannot be merged until coverage is restored.

Similarly, if we want to updatie the GitHub Actions Workflow, for which, we open the **.github/workflows/ci.yml** (from the previous topic), and update the test step:

```
- name: Run unit and integration tests with coverage
  run: pytest --cov=app --cov-fail-under=85 --cov-report=term
--cov-report=xml tests/
```

In the above, the **--cov-report=xml** is useful if you want to upload coverage results to external services (like Codecov or Coveralls) for history tracking and badge generation.

Just to conclude, by integrating **coverage.py** into our test suite, generating actionable HTML reports, and enforcing coverage thresholds in CI, you elevate our project's quality bar, and make test-driven confidence part of our culture, not just our tooling.

Summary

To sum it up, we made sure our software delivery process is reliable by adding solid testing and automation to every step of the process. We started by building unit tests with Pytest, creating both simple and complex test cases, and using fixtures to manage setup and teardown with clarity and repeatability. We used mocking to separate external dependencies, making sure tests were fast and consistent. Integration testing really boosted our confidence.

We used Docker Compose to orchestrate real Redis containers, executed full API request flows, and validated cross-service data consistency. We integrated GitHub Actions pipelines to automate linting, test execution, Docker image building, and secure image pushes to a registry. This establishes a transparent and reproducible path from code change to deployable artifact. Adding coverage reporting made things more consistent, and it allowed us to measure, visualize, and enforce minimum standards for test completeness. We made sure that every new commit kept the project's quality up or even improved it using HTML coverage reports and CI gates. These tools and practices really reinforced the culture we need for modern software — one of accountability, speed, and resilience. They've given us a plan for how to keep up our quality assurance as our codebase and ambitions grow.

Index

G

H

I

J

K

L

M

N

O

P

Thank You

www.ingramcontent.com/pod-product-compliance
Lightning Source LLC
Chambersburg PA
CBHW080213170726
48282CB00030B/1099
9789349174153